IMAGES
of America

OLD WEST BALTIMORE

ON THE COVER: This is a c. 1920s image of Percy Glascoe and His Plantation Orchestra in Baltimore, Maryland. (Courtesy of Nanny Jack & Co. archives.)

IMAGES
of America

OLD WEST BALTIMORE

Philip Jackson Merrill

ARCADIA
PUBLISHING

Published by Arcadia Publishing
Charleston, South Carolina

Printed in the United States of America

Library of Congress Control Number: 2020942315

For all general information, please contact Arcadia Publishing:
Telephone 843-853-2070
Fax 843-853-0044
E-mail sales@arcadiapublishing.com
For customer service and orders:
Toll-Free 1-888-313-2665

Visit us on the Internet at www.arcadiapublishing.com

*To all the people living and deceased who worked hard
to create a thriving community in the face of structural
racism, discrimination, and Jim Crow.*

CONTENTS

ACKNOWLEDGMENTS

First and foremost, I thank God for planting the seed for this project and rendering unto me an unparalleled archive that provided everything needed to complete it.

Also, it is with sincere gratitude that I thank my loved ones: my great-grandmother Gertrude B. Jackson, also known as "Nanny Jack" in her historic Sandtown neighborhood of Old West Baltimore, it was at her breast, on her lap, at her knee, and by her side in our family home that I learned to value and collect the wisdom of age and the stories of artifacts, people, and things around me; my late father, Rev. George B. Merrill, who toiled in the vineyards with us on many history projects; my mother, Betty Louise Merrill, who pioneered and paved the way for all of our family pursuits and successes and continues to be the inspiration and ultimate shining light; Veronica A. Carr, digital media strategist and staff writer for Nanny Jack & Co. LLC, as well as my life partner, whose tireless work ethic and dedication in helping me preserve Old West Baltimore's history is unmatched; and my faithful, lifelong friend Ricky Boots.

In addition, I sincerely thank the following individuals who have contributed their stories, assistance, and research efforts: Marion McGaskey-Blackwell, founder of Historic Marble Hill in Old West Baltimore; Norma and Joyce Green; Danny Marrow; Herb and Shirley Weimar; Bill Jessup; Semuel and his late wife, Audrey Stubbs May; Rob Schoeberlein, acting archivist at the Baltimore City Archives; Eva Slezak of the Enoch Pratt Free Library; and Donna Hollie and Glenn Blackwell of the Agnes Kane Callum Chapter of the Afro-American Historical and Genealogical Society.

Finally, I acknowledge with gratitude these various groups where I was fortunate to serve as a board member: Baltimore City Commission for Historical and Architectural Preservation, Baltimore City Historical Society, Baltimore Heritage, Baltimore National Heritage Area, and Maryland Historical Society's Library Committee, where I served as a member.

All images are courtesy of Nanny Jack & Co. archives.

INTRODUCTION

My people are destroyed for lack of knowledge.

Hosea 4:6

I am proud to be a native son of Sandtown, one of five historic neighborhoods in the largest urban African American district in the National Register of Historic Places. My childhood memories and experiences of this vibrant neighborhood helped to shape my understanding of the true definition of community. Everyone in the neighborhood knew the matriarch of our family, Gertrude B. Jackson, Nanny Jack. I cannot remember a time when our house at 1307 North Stockton Street was not bustling with family, friends, and sometimes strangers in need. Fond memories remain etched in my mind, such as walking with my beloved Nanny Jack to the Lafayette Market at 1700 Pennsylvania Avenue, now the Pennsylvania Avenue Market, and my mother taking me to Mewborn's (Toes') Barber Shop, 634 Laurens Street, to get my hair cut. As a fashionably dressed, outgoing, and highly talkative little fellow, the larger community embraced me and made me feel special. Interacting with the fascinating adult men was always an eye-opening and educational experience for this little boy. Occasionally, when Mom and I would attend Bethel AME Church at 1300 Druid Hill Avenue, even Rev. Frank Madison Reid Sr., who would always talk with attendees after service, had something special to say to me.

Before 2004, when historians, scholars, and researchers thought of urban renaissances in African American communities, it was Harlem in New York, Jackson Ward in Richmond, Bronzeville District in Chicago, U Street in Washington, and Beale Street in Memphis that came to mind. It was not until after the 2004 Baltimore Commission for Historical and Architectural Preservation's inclusion of Old West Baltimore in the National Register of Historic Places that the renaissance in Baltimore's thriving Jim Crow district was included in the conversation.

The historic designation, however, shortchanged the larger significance of five different black neighborhoods by grouping them together under one entity. These distinctively and culturally different neighborhoods—Upton, Druid Heights, Sandtown, Harlem Park, and Madison Park—are each worthy of having their own designation. Within the district are so many different themes in need of proper research and documentation, that a book series is actually warranted. For example, in 2020, Pennsylvania Avenue, the economic and cultural hub of the district, received designation as a black arts and entertainment district. The history of this cultural thoroughfare could easily be its own book, perhaps even several.

It is an arduous and difficult task to document the cultural significance of the buildings, people, events, and the national and international figures who visited, especially since traditionally, the historic preservation groups have mainly focused on the architecture. The National Register defines a historic district as "a geographically definable area—urban or rural, large or small—possessing a significant concentration, linkage, or continuity of sites, buildings, structures, and/or objects united by past events or aesthetically pleasing by plan or physical development." I chose, however, to focus on the significance of the real community: the people, their activities, their connectivity, and their contributions to society, rather than on the significance of the architecture, which is the focus of many white preservationists.

Over the last 30 years, I have worked diligently to build Nanny Jack & Co.'s archives with primary source material to reflect different aspects of the community, such as commercial studio photographs of both everyday and prominent citizens as well as vernacular images. Realistically, the significant role of primary source material is not to be underrated but to be celebrated. While I am fortunate to have acquired this content, it is an ongoing, laborious task to properly interpret and accurately connect it to the community. Identifying African American photographers is difficult because there is no comprehensive database in any state repository. This same struggle applies to the identification and location of the various schools and the understanding of when a school was identified solely by its number and when it received a name. Some of the readers of this book will only remember their school number and not its name. Attempting to research and document church history is equally difficult, if not more, because the churches often have scant records that are not accessible. Some of my church content is unique, and if it has not been documented in a church program or newspaper article, there is no supporting or collaborative information. Mortgage burning programs, anniversary booklets, fundraising tickets, and funeral programs are very important in preserving church history and were heavily utilized.

Although Pennsylvania Avenue was a famed "chitlin circuit" stop and an economic and cultural mecca of the community, the scarcity of its records surpasses all the other topics. Many readers are familiar with the iconic Royal Theatre as being a landmark on the avenue. I have attempted to expand that narrative through business cards, matchbooks, receipts, nightclub souvenir photographs, and directories. This book highlights the evolution of the avenue through various decades and multiple businesses, which often changed names and occupied the same address at different times. For example, the Savoy Night Club in the 1400 block of Pennsylvania Avenue later became the Comedy Club.

Adding to the difficulty of this was the emerging COVID-19 pandemic, which prevented physical visits to important repositories with special collections that could have assisted with the research. For example, institutions such as the Baltimore City Archives, the Maryland Historical Society, the sixth-floor Liber Folio room of the Clarence M. Mitchell Courthouse the *Afro-American* newspaper archives, the Enoch Pratt Free Library, the Commission for Historical and Architectural Preservation Planning Library, the Maryland State Archives, and churches were not open to the public. This restricted me to selecting content from my archives.

In addition, the pandemic prevented me from including chapters on the community's athletic legacy, the overwhelming number of business, social, and cultural clubs that emerged during Jim Crow, and the list of prominent individuals who visited the community because of connections to the various families, churches, businesses, and organizations.

While this book is just a snapshot of the vast experiences that occurred within the district, hopefully, it will be an appetizer for more.

One

CREATING BLACK WEALTH

The *Afro-American Ledger*, which was established in 1892 by formerly enslaved John Henry Murphy Sr., was the leading voice of the African American community. The paper was the product of a merger of two previous publications: the *Ledger*, published by Rev. George F. Bragg, pastor of Baltimore's St. James Episcopal Church, and the *Afro-American*, published by Rev. Dr. William M. Alexander, pastor of Baltimore's Sharon Baptist Church. In 1916, the name of the publication was changed to the *Afro-American*. It is the oldest continuously black family–owned and –operated newspaper. Although the newspaper was located in the historic Seton Hill District, the family lived in Old West Baltimore on Druid Hill Avenue, Myrtle Avenue, and McCulloh Street. Pictured here at right is Carl J. Murphy, son of *Ledger* founder John H. Murphy Sr., with his new bride, Vashti Turley, one of the founders of the Delta Sigma Theta sorority.

Founded in 1903 by philanthropist Harry O. Wilson Sr., Dr. Charles H. Fowler, and Minnie B. Lewis, the Mutual Benefit Society provided weekly life insurance and accident, sickness, and death benefits to African Americans. The business also employed generations of black underwriters who lived in the district. The company had a great marketing strategy with products like souvenir matchbooks (above), flyswatters, fans, publications (right), postcards of the building, and assorted promotional giveaways. At one point in his life, Wilson lived in the 1600 block of Division Street and was an active member and strong financial supporter of Trinity Baptist Church.

INSURE TODAY the MUTUAL WAY

MUTUAL BENEFIT NEWS

SPECIAL ♥ ANNIVERSARY EDITION

VOL. 1   BALTIMORE, MD., MAY, 1940   NO. 4

MUTUAL'S CELEBRATION IN FULL SWING

STORY OF MUTUAL'S GROWTH TOLD

The Mutual, now celebrating its 37th Anniversary, was founded by Harry O. Wilson, with the aid of Charles H. Fowler and Mrs. Minnie B. Lewis on May 3, 1903, as a mere fraternal benefit society.

Only one room was first occupied by the company, and the receipts for the initial year amounted to only $864.60.

The budding organization was confronted by many obstacles and problems, but hard work, perseverance and careful management enabled the company to weather the difficulties caused by the great Baltimore fire, the "flu" epidemic and the recent economic depression. Moreover, the Mutual was destined to help the Maryland Negro buy homes and churches, employ his children, and safeguard his loved ones in time of sickness and death.

Today, the Mutual enjoys an exceptional record and is lauded for its unselfish service to humanity—its strength and stability. It is truly a "Mutual Benefit" Society.

(Continued on Page 2)

FIRST PRESIDENT

The late Dr. Charles E. Fowler, the first President of the Mutual and one of Maryland's first and most prominent physicians.

AT HER DESK

Mrs. Minnie B. _____, _____, Vice-President of the Mutual, is loved and respected by all employees.

U. S. FUNERAL DIRECTORS EARN $6,000,000

In the United States, 1,458 establishments operated by Negro funeral directors, embalmers and operators of crematories, realized receipts amounting to $6,949,000. They give employment to 2,385 full-time and part-time employees with payments amounting to $1,223,000.

The Colored Funeral Directors Association of Maryland, Inc., includes in its membership representatives who have up to date equipment, and who enjoy a reputation of giving dignified and personal service. Officers of the C. F. D. A. are as follows: John M. Johnson, President; Eugene Payne, Rec. Secretary; Robert L. Young, Fin. Secretary; James W. S_____, _____.

Printing Dept.'s New Automatic

The efficiency of _____ Mutual's Printing Department _____ _____ increased with the installation of an automatic press, a Miehle Vertical.

Carroll Jones, printer, says the press is capable of making 3800 impressions per hour; and through its design, virtually eliminates vibration and minimizes wear.

37th YEAR MARK PRAISED BY PUBLIC

The Mutual Benefit Society's celebration of its 37th Anniversary began full swing Monday, April 29th. Festivities will continue until May 11th.

Policyholders, public officials and friends, all over the state, are sending messages of praise. Mutual officials are delighted over the progress made in so short a time.

Special Sunday messages have been promised, radio announcements have been planned. A big contest especially held for all the school children of the state is under way. $100.00 in prizes for employees have been posted, and Mutual agents are knocking on every door, getting the new applications that have been promised.

_____ plan to _____ _____ _____ _____ being circulated. The Mutual Heart is sweeping the state, and plans are made to issue more. The public is invited to visit during Open House on May 3rd, at which time a flower show may be presented, and the

(Continued on Page 2)

FOUNDER

The late Harry O. Wilson, Founder, President and General Manager of the Mutual, also managed a bank, two building associations and a Christmas Club.

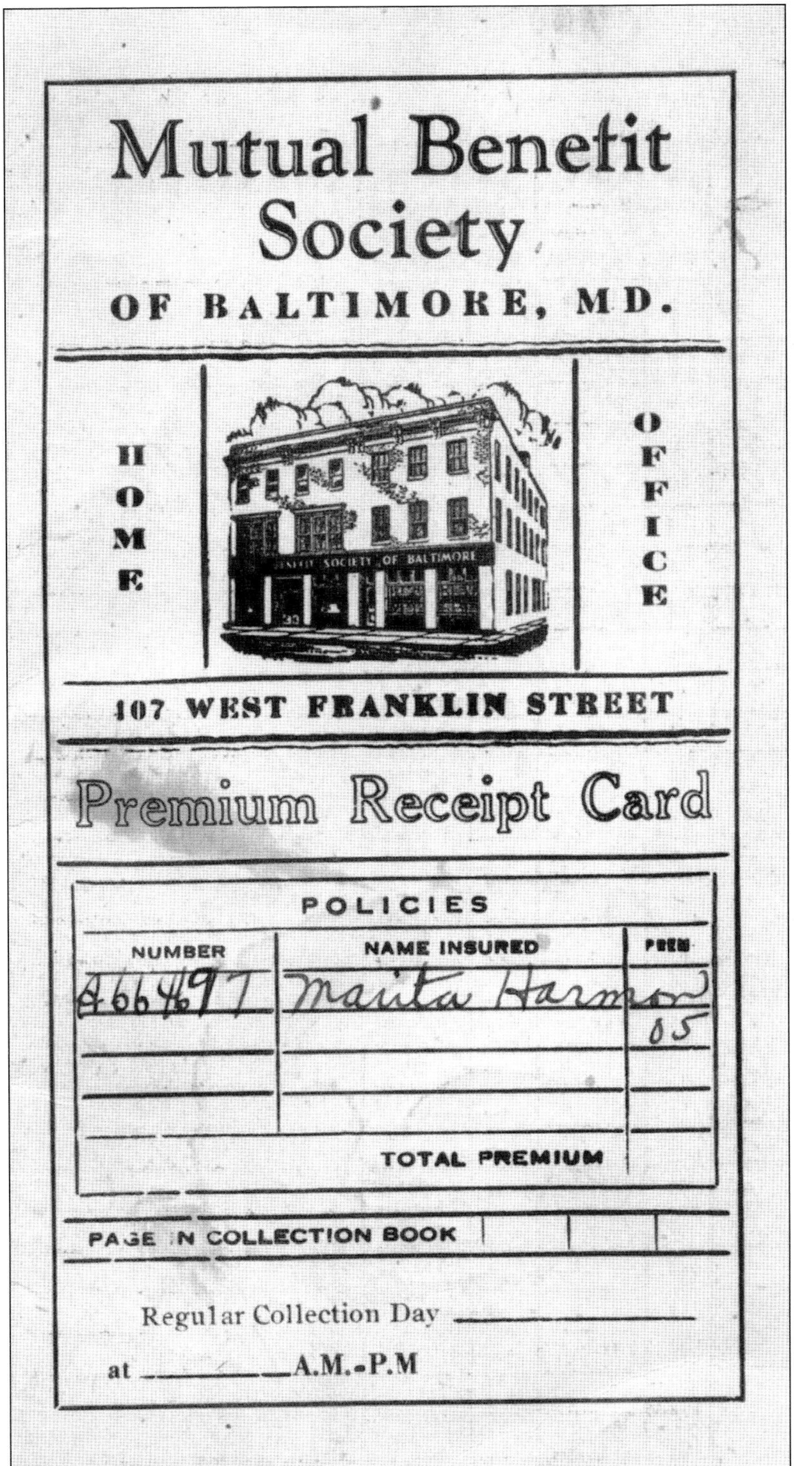

Mutual Benefit Society
OF BALTIMORE, MD.

H O M E

O F F I C E

107 WEST FRANKLIN STREET

Premium Receipt Card

POLICIES

NUMBER	NAME INSURED	PREM
466497	*Maita Harmon*	0 5
	TOTAL PREMIUM	

PAGE IN COLLECTION BOOK

Regular Collection Day _____

at _____A.M.-P.M

Once the company expanded, some customers would go to Wilson's private residence in Wilson Park, an African American community developed by Wilson, to pay their weekly premiums.

Thomas R. Smith had numerous nicknames penned by both the African American and white press, but the most famous one was "the Unofficial Black Mayor of Baltimore." From the 1890s until his death in 1938, Smith operated Smith's Hotel with his brother Wallace and owned at least 12 other businesses. His hotel was well known throughout the country, and prominent musicians, athletes, politicians, and others stayed there. Smith was a noted Democratic political boss who helped to rig elections in favor of the Democratic party. His power and influence were far-reaching and included churches, schools, housing, police, politicians, and gambling. From 1912 until 1932, Smith and his wife, Jessie, lived at 2035 Druid Hill Avenue.

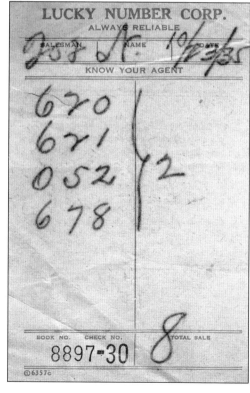

Thomas R. Smith also owned the Lucky Number Corp., one of numerous illegal lottery rackets in Baltimore. For many years, the number chosen was the last three digits of "the handle," the amount that race track bettors placed on race days at major tracks like Baltimore's Pimlico. If one was lucky enough to hit that number, they would receive a payout. The lottery employed men, women, and children, frequently referred to as "number runners," and they worked out of every possible location, including private residences, beauty salons, the old Lafayette Market, and white-owned businesses. This 1935 number receipt is from a noted family on McCulloh Street.

George M. Lane was a late-19th-century attorney and reportedly the first African American to run as a mayoral candidate. Lane was also one of the first African Americans admitted to the Maryland Bar and was a founder of the Lexington Savings Bank at 314 North Eutaw Street. For a brief time, he resided in the 1600 block of Division Street with his wife and children. He was the father of pioneering judge E. Everett Lane. This distinguished portrait was captured by noted black photographer John Jones.

Attorney William Norman Bishop attended Yale Law School in Connecticut; he did not graduate but was able to pass both the Connecticut and Maryland Bars. Bishop was a charter member of the Delta Lambda Chapter of Alpha Phi Alpha fraternity. He was descended from a prominent pre–Civil War Maryland family. Bishop also operated a funeral parlor with his father, John A. Bishop, from the family residences in the 1100 block of Druid Hill Avenue and the 1200 block of McCulloh Street.

James Steward Davis was an early African American graduate of Dickinson Law School in Carlisle, Pennsylvania. During the 1920s, he was a highly respected trial lawyer in Baltimore who represented both black and white clients. At one point, he partnered with attorney and funeral parlor operator William Norman Bishop, and the two had an uptown office at 1107 Druid Hill Avenue. Davis was Bishop's only law partner.

Prominent attorney James Steward Davis lived with the Bishop family in the 1200 block of McCulloh Street before his 1920 marriage to educator Blanche Moore. In April 1929, Davis departed from Baltimore, foregoing his practice, wife, and children, and was never seen again. For 10 years, the *Afro-American* newspaper published articles about Davis's disappearance.

Provident Hospital, an African American–owned and –operated hospital and nursing school, was established in 1894 in the 400 block of Orchard Street. In October 1928, the Provident Hospital and Free Dispensary moved to the 1500 block of Division Street, pictured in this pamphlet. The building was constructed by Albert Irvin Cassell, a noted black architect. Cassell was a graduate of Baltimore's Colored High School, which was within walking distance of the hospital.

PROVIDENT HOSPITAL, INC.

Many of Provident Hospital's nurses, doctors, and staff lived in the district, and one way of keeping the larger community engaged was through the *Provident Hospital Bulletin*. This is a May-June 1940 copy of the bulletin, which could be purchased for 10¢ a copy or a $1 yearly subscription.

Provident Hospital was constantly raising funds through various charitable activities. A segregated women's group called Just Us Girls hosted a Louis Armstrong and His Combo charity dance, along with other notable musicians listed on the cover of this program. The program includes photographs and information about various aspects of the hospital and advertisements for local businesses.

Hod carriers were laborers employed in carrying supplies to bricklayers, stonemasons, cement finishers, or plasterers on the job. These eight men were likely members of the Local 194 of the Hod Carriers & Laborers union. They worked on buildings throughout Baltimore City, and the African American union members often donated money to other local black institutions, including Provident Hospital.

LOCAL 194
A.F. OF L.
STEWARD
212
HOD CARRIERS. & LABORERS

17

State Board of Undertakers

of Maryland

This Certifies That __Mrs. Helen A. Holland**__
has been duly licensed to practice Undertaking in
MARYLAND for the year ending APRIL 30th, 1927.

HENRY W. MEARS, President.

H. H. HOUSMAN, Jr., Secretary.

Mrs. Helen V. Holland

Signature of Licensee.

Funeral Services

of the late

Helen Augusta Gibson Holland

in the Sanctuary of

Bethel A. M. E. Church

Thursday, January 15, 1959 — 11:00 a. m.

The Reverend Harrison J. Bryant, Minister

The Reverend I. Alphonso Miller, Minister to the Deceased

Helen A. Holland and her husband, George, operated Holland's Funeral Home in the 1600 block of Druid Hill Avenue. Holland was able to continue her late husband's business after his 1923 death. With the assistance of her brother George T. Gibson Jr., she secured a state license in 1927. She was a respected funeral home operator in the community for over 30 years and conducted the funerals for thousands of black Baltimoreans. She also gave an apprenticeship to Herbert Nutter, who later opened the Nutter Funeral Home and named the Helen Holland Chapel in her honor.

In 1872, Rev. James Peck and other trustees of the Sharp Street Church established Mount Auburn Cemetery in the historic Mount Winans community. Their offices were in the 1200 block of Etting Street, also known as the Sharp Street Community House, within the district. The cemetery was dedicated as a Baltimore city historic landmark in 1986. Notable people such as Joe Gans, W. Ashbie Hawkins, John H. Murphy Sr., Lillie Carroll Jackson, Thomas R. Smith, and Percy Glascoe, as well as formerly enslaved people and soldiers, are buried there. The cemetery is also known as "the City of the Dead for Colored People." This 1914 deed is for a $20 cemetery plot for Henry W. Campbell.

This 1920s photograph shows Stewart family headstones at Mount Auburn. The Stewarts were relatives of the Weaver family, early members of Trinity Baptist Church and longtime residents of the district. The Weavers eventually lived in the 1300 block of Druid Hill Avenue.

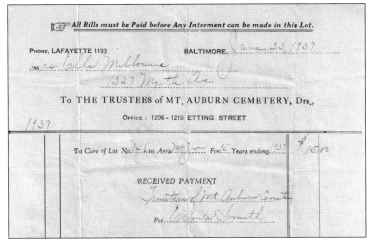

This 1937 receipt shows Ella Milbourne's payment of $15 for perpetual care of a Mount Auburn plot. Perpetual care and other maintenance issues have plagued the cemetery for generations.

The Monumental Lodge No. 3 is in the 1500 block of Madison Avenue. African American realtor and musician Robert J. Young sold this property to the Elks in 1925. The lodge was home to many prominent Elks and leaders such as George W.F. McMechen, Thomas R. Smith, Roy S. Bond, Josiah F. Henry Jr., and John H. Murphy Jr. The Elks participated in mass protests, boycotts, lobbying campaigns, and voter registration drives. Established in 1900, it is the oldest fraternal lodge of the Improved Benevolent and Protective Order of Elks of the World in Baltimore. This 1925 certificate for George W. Mason is for one $5 share in the lodge.

In 1922, James Finley Wilson was elected as the grand exalted ruler of the Elks and remained in this position for over 25 years. Although he was from Washington, DC, Finley had strong ties to Monumental Lodge No. 3 and also founded the *Baltimore Times* newspaper. During his tenure, he increased the Elks' national membership from 30,000 to 500,000 and oversaw the creation of over 900 new lodges.

The August 1936 Elks convention was held in New York. From left to right are Donald Brown, Miss Robinson, Laura Collier, and Elks member Robert Collier on top of the Empire State Building. The Colliers lived in the 1100 block of North Carey Street and were longtime members of Payne Memorial AME Church, both within the district.

MASONIC TEMPLE
McCULLOH & MOSHER
BALTO. MD.

PHOTO BY
LANE
1631 PENN.
Av.

The Mount Lebanon Lodge No. 22 of the Free and Accepted Masons, at the corner of McCulloh and Mosher Streets, was photographed by noted African American photographer Early G. Lane of Druid Hill Avenue. The lodge was in the First Masonic District. Many of the Masons lived, worked, and were active within the district, such as Worshipful Grand Master Willard W. Allen and lodge secretary Charles T. Gilles.

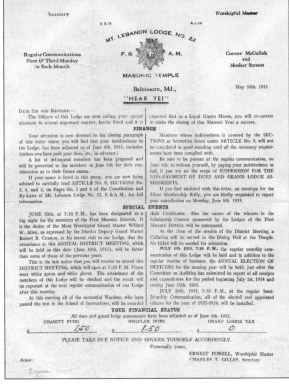

Charles T. Gilles is seen here in a portrait by African American photographer Arthur L. Macbeth. Gilles worked as a custodian for many years at Douglass High School.

Sess' Restaurant, in the 1600 block of Division Street, was an African American family–owned and –operated restaurant. It opened during the World War II–era and remained in business for over 40 years. The restaurant was operated by William and Manzella Sessoms, their daughter Louise, and valued employees. Noted black photographer E. Victor Wright captured this image of the building.

MENU

SESS' Restaurant
1639 Division St. (corner of Wilson)
BALTIMORE, MD.

PLASTIC MENU COVERS BY RISCH P. O. BOX 567, ROCHESTER 2, N. Y.

The Sessoms family lived in the 1900 block of Division Street and were a prime example of an entrepreneurial family that lived and worked within the community and made it sustainable. Many celebrities dined at Sess', including heavyweight boxing champion Joe "the Brown Bomber" Louis, Duke Ellington, and Count Basie. Prominent politicians, businessmen, and high school students also dined there. The restaurant was well-known for its delicious liver and onions.

Frank A. Simmons's skill as a painter, decorator, and landscaper allowed him to have both African American and white customers throughout Baltimore, particularly within the district. His clientele included commercial businesses, like the *Afro-American* newspaper, as well as private residences. He kept an ad in the *Afro-American* for years. His headquarters and home address was in the 1900 block of Druid Hill Avenue. Simmons was active with the Josephite Catholic community and was close friends with Fr. Charles Randolph Uncles. On his business card, Simmons listed that he was a member of the Association for the Promotion of Negro Business.

PHONE, MADISON 8747   MEMBER OF A. P. N. B.

Frank A. Simmons

PAINTER AND DECORATOR

FLOORS RE-SURFACED AND FINISHED

1932 DRUID HILL AVENUE   BALTIMORE, MD.

The Ideal Building and Loan Association was founded by Teackle Wallis Lansey in 1920 in the 1600 block of Druid Hill Avenue. It was established to help African American families secure mortgage loans to purchase homes in Baltimore. The association was open on Thursday nights to serve those customers who were household staff, like cooks or maids, of white families because this was the one night of the week that they were given time off. At one point, it was the longest continuously black family–owned bank in Maryland. The building was near other important businesses, such as the Colored YMCA, Holland Funeral Home, and Druid Laundry. This booklet belonged to Clarence and Juanita Jackson Mitchell, lawyers and civil rights activists.

Mr. & Mrs. Clarence M. Mitchell, Jr.
1239 Druid hill Avenue
Baltimore, Md. 21217

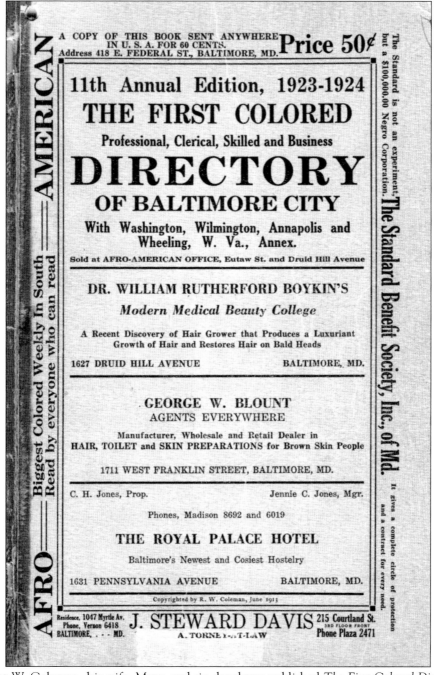

Robert W. Coleman, his wife, Mary, and six daughters published *The First Colored Directory of Baltimore City* from 1913 until Coleman's death in 1946 from their home in the 1100 block of Myrtle Avenue. The Coleman directory, like the 1923–1924 one pictured here, provided an excellent source for documenting the African American community. Often referred to as the "blue book," the directory had advertisements for a variety of black businesses in Baltimore and offered biographical sketches of prominent black citizens. Coleman, who was blind, also established the Maryland Association for the Colored Blind, which became the Association for the Handicapped.

Association *of* Colored Municipal Employees

OF BALTIMORE, INC.

1629 DRUID HILL AVENUE
BALTIMORE - 17, MD.

TO: MEMBERS OF ASSOCIATION OF COLORED MUNICIPAL EMPLOYEES OF BALTIMORE, INC.

This is one of the extra services that your Association of Colored Employees of Baltimore, Inc. gives you!

Your Association of Colored Municipal Employees of Baltimore, Inc. has arranged with CONSUMER'S BUYING ASSOCIATION for you to purchase all your home needs at some of the largest discounts in Baltimore.

Minimum - 20% on all Appliances (Television, Refrigerators, etc.).

Minimum - 25% up to 40% on all Furniture.

The CONSUMER'S BUYING ASSOCIATION, who give you this privilege, sell all Nationally famous brands of Furniture (Bedroom, Living room, Dining room and Kitchen), Rugs, Mirrors, Lamps, Mattresses, Springs Chairs, Tables, etc., as well as Television Sets (all makes and models), Refrigerators, Gas Ranges, Washing Machines, Sewing Machines and all other Home Appliances and Home Needs.

The procedure is very simple. You go to CONSUMER'S BUYING ASSOCIATION, 202 N. Pearl St. (at W. Lexington St. ½ block below Paca) and select any home furnishing you may need. You then present your CBA Discount Card, which you will find enclosed, and the discount will be deducted from your purchase.

The Association of Colored Municipal Employees of Baltimore, Inc. has merely arranged for its members to purchase at a discount, and does not assume responsibility for any of the sales transactions.

Very truly yours,

WILLIAM T. DORSEY
Executive Secretary

P.S. Please fill in your name on the card when you receive it. If you will be interested in a Lionel Train Set or a two-wheel bicycle this Christmas, come in and place a small deposit. This is a hard-to-get item and we do not want to disappoint any of our customers.

PAY THEM A VISIT (AT NO OBLIGATION) AND BE GLAD

DON'T WAIT (OR BUY SOMEWHERE ELSE) AND BE SAD

Daily 9:00 A. M. to 6:00 P. M.
Monday and Thursday 'till 9:00 P. M.

IT PAYS TO INVESTIGATE!

The Association of Colored Municipal Employees, under the leadership of executive secretary William T. Dorsey, allowed those who worked for the government to obtain discounts on home furnishings and other goods through a partnership with the Consumer Buying Association. Their members would present a Consumer Buying Association card to receive the discount. This organization was inside the same building as the Ideal Building and Loan Association, in the 1600 block of Druid Hill Avenue.

Druid Laundry was established in 1896 in the 1600 block of Druid Hill Avenue and was one of two African American–owned laundries in Baltimore. It was owned by educator Harry T. Pratt, longtime principal at Douglass High School. In 1912, he formed a partnership with T. Wallis Lansey, who also owned the Ideal Building and Loan Association across the street from the laundry. By 1938, the business was grossing $40,000 a year, served over 2,000 customers weekly, and employed numerous members within the district. They also had a location outside of the district in the 900 block of Druid Hill Avenue.

The Druid Hill Avenue YMCA was in the 1600 block of Druid Hill Avenue. In 1915, the community worked together to raise funds for a new building in conjunction with philanthropist Julius Rosenwald of Sears, Roebuck and Co. The team captains listed on the left side of the letter below reads like a who's who in the district. The YMCA served as a community center that provided activities for both youth and adults, such as sports, educational, and cultural events. The sign in the window at left reads, "Colored Young Men's Christian Association, Special Men's Meeting, Sunday 4:30 pm, Rev. A.B. Callis, All Men Invited, Bring a friend, Good singing."

NEW BUILDING FOR COLORED MEN AND BOYS

$2,000.00 CASH IN SIXTEEN DAYS

DRUID HILL AVENUE BRANCH

Young Men's Christian Association

November 19th to December 6th, 1915

Headquarters: 1619 Druid Hill Avenue
Phone Madison 1120   Baltimore, Md.   1915

W. ASHBIE HAWKINS, ESQ.
General Chairman

S. S. BOOKER, Secretary

TEAMS & CAPTAINS

DIVISION A
G. W. F. McMECHEN, Chair.
GEO. V. LOTTIER, Sec'y.
W. H. LANGLEY
Dr. B. M. RHETTA
LEWIS E. WILLIAMS
J. EDWARD SMITH

DIVISION B
J. P. EVANS, Chairman
Dr. A. O. Reid, Secretary
THOMAS H. SMITH
SAMUEL P. WILLIAMS
EMERSON HILLEN
DENNIS HALL

DIVISION C
JOHN W. RICH, Chairman
W. A. JONES, Secretary
WM. T. GRIGGS
THOS. F. JONES
GEO. W. HENRY
R. A. FRYE

DIVISION D
Dr. T. S. HAWKINS, Chairman
JAS. A. B. CALLIS, Secretary
DR. W. H. WRIGHT
RALPH V. COOK
J. ARTHUR TURNER
DAN. H. MURPHY

DIVISION E
JAS. W. HUGHES, Chairman
W. S. EMERSON, Secretary
HARRY T. PRATT
Lawyer L. CLARKE SMITH
GEO. B. MURPHY
SOLOMON DeCOURSEY

My dear Subcriber:

You will pardon our anxiety an unusual interest at this time when you know the particulars we wish to present. Your past interest warrant our action and compell us to give you another opportunity to give tangible evidence of your good faith and generous spirit.

As you know, the campaign for the New Y. M. C. A. Building was launched November 18, 1912 at which time 3322 subscribed $51,328.95. $12,975.00 of that amount has been paid to date. The first agreement was that the actual constructions would begin as soon as $15,000 had been paid by the colored people. To meet the first condition, you see we must raise $2025.00.

Knowing that Mr. Rosenwald's offer expires Jan. 1st, 1916, and cancels the whole project unless met by us we deem it our duty to remind you of your pledge and urge you to comply in order to save our good name and reputation.

One of our official collectors will call to see you between November 19th and December 6th. Do not turn him away, but plan to pay your pledge, a part of it, at least. This is our LAST CHANCE. No sacrifice is too great to meet this issue.

We are counting upon you to help win for your city this great enterprise.

Sincerely yours,

W. ASHBIE HAWKINS

S. S. BOOKER

PROGRAM AND DANCE

FOR SOLDIERS IN UNIFORMS

Under auspices of the
UNITED SERVICE ORGANIZATION

At The Druid Hill Avenue—Y. M. C. A.

SATURDAY, MARCH 14, 1942 — 8:00 P. M.

Alpha Sigma Chapter of Zeta Phi Beta Sorority

FEATURING FINER WOMANHOOD WEEK

(This Hostess Card Admits You)

During World War II, the USO held dances at the YMCA to benefit the soldiers.

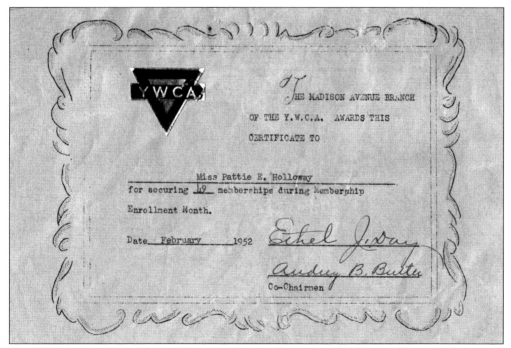

The YWCA was organized in 1897 and was originally in the 1200 block of Druid Hill Avenue. In 1942, the YWCA purchased and moved to the former Baltimore Hebrew Congregation's Synagogue House in the 1900 block of Madison Avenue. During World War II, the organization raised $100,000 to renovate the building. By 1944, the building was fully restored by African American architect Albert Irvin Cassell. The new design created space for 20 permanent residents and 18 shorter-term guests. The holder of the certificate below, Pattie E. Holloway, was very active in raising funds for the YWCA, NAACP, and Provident Hospital, all within her neighborhood.

The Club Astoria, in the 1300 block of Edmondson Avenue, opened in December 1935. The owner, Harold Mason, was a native of the British West Indies and built the club at a cost of $25,000. It was advertised as the "finest musical show bar south of New York." Customers at the Club Astoria were accustomed to hearing the biggest names on the "chitlin circuit," including some who later earned international acclaim. Musicians who performed there included Milton "Tiny" Bradshaw, Ella Fitzgerald, Don Redmon and His Rhythm Kings, Blanche Calloway, Billie Holiday, Detroit Red, and many others. The club was within walking distance of Pennsylvania Avenue.

Educators Rebecca and William Griggs (left) are pictured with friends in this Club Astoria souvenir photograph. Many people had souvenir pictures taken at the club. The club's advertisements proclaimed, "It's smart to be seen at the Astoria Musical Bar."

Many nightclubs within the district provided their patrons with opportunities to purchase souvenir photographs that became great keepsakes.

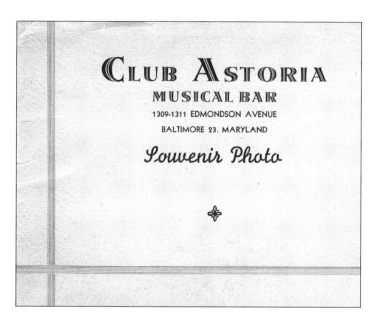

CLUB ASTORIA
MUSICAL BAR
1309-1311 EDMONDSON AVENUE
BALTIMORE 23, MARYLAND

Souvenir Photo

Milton "Tiny" Bradshaw and his orchestra were frequent performers at Club Astoria and were well-known in the district. Bradshaw is second from right. The drummer, third from the right, is attributed as Joe Jones, who performed with many other noted musicians. Bradshaw's biggest hit was "Well, Oh Well" in 1950. Outside of the famed Royal Theatre on Pennsylvania Avenue, the Club Astoria was the second most popular music venue.

Operating from the Fremont Avenue Garage, Diggs Motor Coach provided transportation for hundreds of Baltimore schoolchildren and ran charter trips in the Mid-Atlantic region. The company was started by Herbert Diggs Sr., and his son Robert H. Diggs continued to operate the business until the late 1950s. Robert Diggs, also known as "Bobby," was a graduate of Baltimore's Frederick Douglass High School. This is another example of a business owned and operated by an African American who was a member of the community and whose business served the community.

Henry G. Parks Jr. invested in the launching and expansion of Crayton Southern Sausage Company in Cleveland, Ohio. When Parks disagreed with Leroy Crayton over the company's expansion, he sold his interest in Crayton and moved to Baltimore. He partnered with noted businessman and financier William "Little Willie" Adams and founded Parks Sausage in 1951. The company's first location was in an abandoned dairy plant at the corner of Pennsylvania and North Avenues. The company employed many African Americans in the district, and their slogan, "More Parks' Sausages, Mom," became a nationwide sensation. By 1955, the company was a major sponsor of the World Series. In 1969, it was the first African American company to go public on Wall Street.

Two

Pennsylvania Avenue Main Street

The Douglass Theater in the 1300 block of Pennsylvania Avenue was renamed the Royal Theatre in 1925. It hosted a number of entertainers, including Ethel Waters, Louis Armstrong, Jimmie Lunceford, Bessie Smith, Fats Waller, Duke Ellington, Princess Wee Wee, the Whitman Sisters, and many others. Clockwise from top left in this 1940s montage are signs for the Royal Theatre and Strand Bowling; child prodigy Sugar Chile Robinson with an unidentified man; two unidentified performers; and renowned gospel singer Sister Rosetta Tharpe. At center is bandleader Lucky Millinder (left) and two performers. The collage was done by African American photographer Gordon "Doc" Anderson, who lived in the 700 block of North Carey Street. Anderson sat in the front row of every Royal show every week and shot everything. He would then print the pictures in his signature montage style and sell them to the artists. Anderson left Baltimore to perform the same job at New York's famed Apollo Theater.

ED 2031

DECCA RECORDS | Billie Holiday
Vol. 1

Easy Living

•

What Is This Thing Called Love

•

Them There Eyes

•

God Bless' the Child

EXTENDED **45** PLAY

Billie Holiday, born in Philadelphia as Eleanora Fagan, spent her childhood in Baltimore. Around 1930, she renamed herself Billie Holiday after film star Billie Dove. At the age of 18, she was discovered by producer John Hammond while singing in a Harlem club. She received the nickname "Lady Day" from friend and music partner Lester "Prez" Young in 1937. Holiday frequently performed at the Royal Theatre and the Club Astoria. In 1938, she recorded her most famous song, "Strange Fruit," about the lynchings of African Americans. The autograph on this album cover reads, "For Shirley, Stay Happy. Billie Holiday."

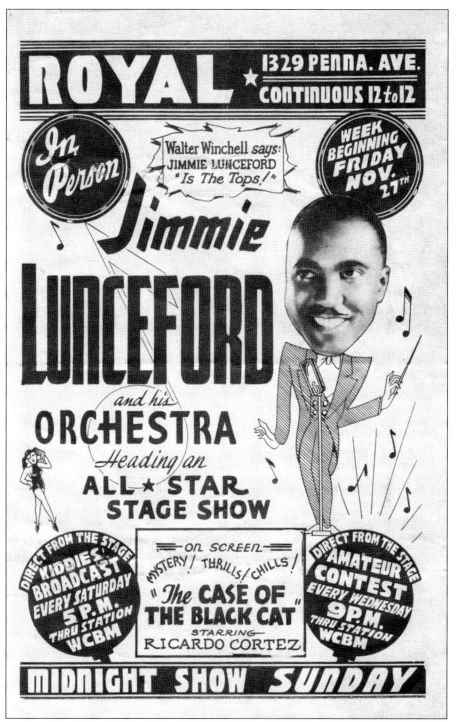

Jimmie Lunceford formed his orchestra in 1927, and by 1935, it was one of the top African American swing bands. This advertisement was from his November 1936 appearance at the Royal Theatre alongside blues singer Bessie Smith, where he performed his song "Harlem Shout." Lunceford also appeared at the Strand Ballroom next to the Royal Theatre.

Blanche Calloway was a singer, bandleader, composer, and pioneering radio disc jockey. The older sister of Cab Calloway, she paved the way for him to enter the music industry. Born in New York, she moved with her family to Baltimore between 1912 and 1913. Her mother, Eulalia, was a gifted musician and encouraged Blanche to take voice and piano lessons. Blanche performed in local choir concerts at Grace Presbyterian Church on Dolphin and Etting Streets in the district. In 1921, she made her professional debut with Noble Sissle and Eubie Blake's musical *Shuffle Along.* She was one of the earliest women to front an all-male band, Blanche Calloway and Her Joy Boys. Blanche frequently performed at the Royal Theatre and the Club Astoria.

Cabell "Cab" Calloway III was born in Rochester, New York, into a musically gifted family. His older sister Blanche was a singer, bandleader, and composer, and his mother, Eulalia, was a pianist. Between 1912 and 1913, the family moved to Baltimore and lived at several properties throughout the city, including the 2200 block of Druid Hill Avenue. Cab graduated from Douglass High School, where he and his sister were students of music teacher and composer William Llewellyn Wilson. He and his orchestra toured the United States, Canada, and Europe and frequently performed at the Royal Theatre. Cab Calloway's *Hepsters Dictionary* was originally published in 1938 and was reprinted several times. The 1944 edition included terms such as "hincty," which meant snooty, and "lay some iron," which meant tap dance. Many of these terms were used in his songs.

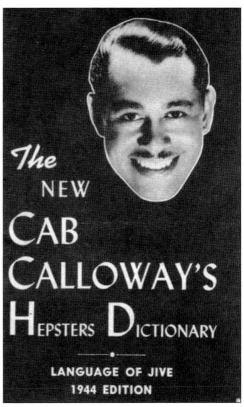

Born as Laura Livingstone, Detroit Red was a dancer and singer who often dressed as a man for her performances. She was given her nickname by comedian Speedy Smith, who called her "Detroit" to distinguish her from all the other red-headed girls in his show. Before going into show business, Livingstone was an undertaker's assistant and a professional embalmer. Early in her stage career, she was one of the stars of Irvin C. Miller's Brown Skin Models. In 1928, she befriended singer Billie Holiday, and the two remained friends until Holiday's death. Detroit Red frequently performed at the Club Astoria and the Royal Theatre. This photograph was signed in May 1936 to a Mr. and Mrs. Perkins when Detroit Red performed at the Club Astoria.

Harriet Thompson was born in Pennsylvania. Her family moved to Baltimore shortly after her birth, where they resided in the 1700 block of Presstman Street. At an early age, she entered show business as a dancer and performed under the stage name "Princess Wee Wee" because of her small stature. During her career, she danced before two US presidents and various European royalty. Starting in 1925, she toured as a featured dancer with the Whitman Sisters, and in January 1931, she performed with them at the Royal Theatre.

Pictured here at the drums, William Henry "Chick" Webb was born in Baltimore. As a young child, he suffered from spinal tuberculosis, which caused him to be short. He dropped out of school and worked odd jobs, including selling newspapers. With the money he earned, he purchased a drum set and began performing with local groups. He joined Percy Glascoe's Jazzola Orchestra, where he played alongside Baltimore-born banjo and guitar player John Truehart aboard Chesapeake Bay steamers. Webb frequently performed along Pennsylvania Avenue at the New Albert Auditorium in the 1200 block, the Strand Ballroom, and the Royal Theatre.

Percy Glascoe, at far right, was the leader of the Plantation Orchestra. The band played at several Pennsylvania Avenue venues, including the New Albert Auditorium, the Strand Ballroom, and the Savoy Ballroom in the 1400 block. When Glascoe died in 1933, his spot as bandleader was filled by James Edward "Bubby" Johnson (second from right). Johnson also served as the vice president of the Musicians' Protective Union, Local No. 543. Glascoe, Johnson, Ike Dixon, and Bob Young fronted various bands with different names and members over the years.

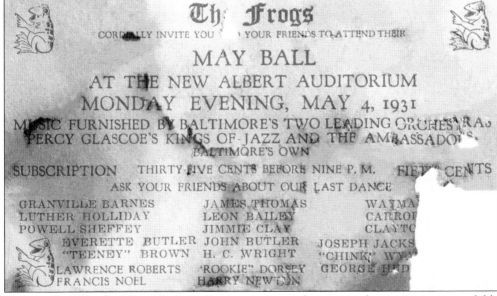

In the early 1930s, the New Albert Auditorium was one of many popular music venues available for performances. The Frogs, an African American charitable organization, hosted a May Ball in May 1931, where Percy Glascoe's Kings of Jazz and the Ambassadors performed.

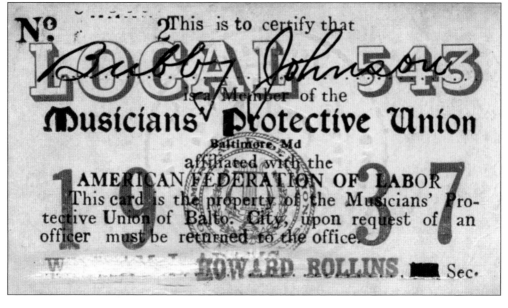

The Musician's Protective Union Local No. 543 was an African American music union organized in Baltimore in 1918 because of exclusion from white music unions. James "Bubby" Johnson, leader of Bubby Johnson's Plantation Orchestra, was vice president of the union at one point. Each member was given a copy of the constitution and bylaws and was required to pay union dues. Musicians in the union could only play with those who were also union members.

Musicians Protective Association

LOCAL UNION NO. 543 A. F. OF M, BALTIMORE, MD.

Contract Blank for Bubby Johnson's
Plantation Orchestra

Baltimore, Md. ....*Nov 2nd*.... 19.**56**

The undersigned, as party of the first part and second part respectively as follows:

The party of the first part agrees to furnish /.**3**..Musicians, members of Local Union No. 543 American Federation of Musicians, AS THEIR AGENT, to the party of the second part, for the sum of $.**85**.**00**...........beng wages for

Dance engagemet Rennert Hotel
On the said Night Fri. Dec. 11th 1936
Time from 9 — 1

Balance Due $.**5.00**.... to be paid at **Intermission** in **small** bills

_____

_____

Bubby Johnson
Party of the First Part

Lambda Sigma Fra. per William Zimmerman
Party of the Second Part

The above contract to be subject to te rules of Local Union No. 543 of the American Federation of Musicians. *524 E. North Ave Ch. 2643*

"All contracts must be filed with the Secretary within one week after the sigr. .ng thereof, and no contract is valid until accepted by the Executive Committee."
As the musieians engaged under the stipulations of this contract are members of the American Fedaration of Musicians nothing in this shall ever be so coustruced as to interfere with any obligation which the musicans owe to the A.F. of M by reason of thier prior obligation to the A. F. of M. as members thereof

The union also negotiated contracts for musicians, like this 1936 contract for Bubby Johnson's Plantation Orchestra, which played at Baltimore's segregated Rennert Hotel for $85.

MADISON 6631 - W.
WILKINS 3073

PEE WEE WOODEN'S
Three Kings And A Queen
(Orchestra and Combo)
MUSIC FOR ALL OCCASIONS

1610 W. NORTH AVE, APT-2   BALTIMORE 17, MD,

Charles "Pee Wee" Wooden's Band was known by several names, including Pee Wee Wooden's Three Kings and A Queen, and featured a female bass player. During the 1950s, the group played in Baltimore, New York, Atlantic City, and Philadelphia clubs. They frequently performed along Pennsylvania Avenue at the Royal Theatre; the Comedy Club in the 1400 block; the Avenue Cafe and Gamby's, both in the 1500 block; Club Ubangi in the 2200 block; and Little Willie's Inn in the 2300 block of Druid Hill Avenue. Wooden is second from right below.

Bessie Smith began singing at a young age and came under the tutelage of blues vocalist Ma Rainey. In 1923, Smith signed a contract with Columbia Records, and that December, she performed at Baltimore's Douglass Theatre, renamed the Royal Theatre in 1925. She was one of the highest-paid performers of the 1920s, which earned her the nickname "the Empress of the Blues." This image is from a real photo postcard made by the African American Williams Studio in the 1500 block of Pennsylvania Avenue.

Ethel Llewellyn Ennis was born in Baltimore and began playing piano at Frederick Douglass High School. However, her vocal talent soon eclipsed her piano playing, and after graduation, she toured with artists such as Louis Armstrong, Benny Goodman, Count Basie, and others. Ennis was featured on the cover of the November 1957 edition of *Pub* magazine, an African American–owned publication that covered Baltimore's nightlife, music, and sports. Despite her international fame, Ennis chose to remain and perform in Baltimore at locations such as Club Casino in the 1400 block of Pennsylvania Avenue. Her middle name, Llewellyn, was in honor of William Llewellyn Wilson, a longtime music educator and composer in Baltimore's colored school system.

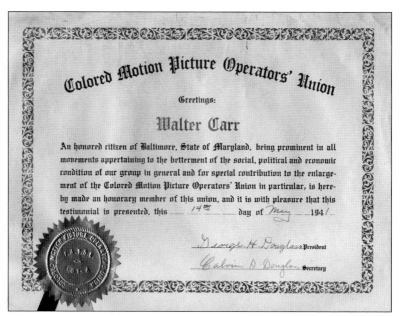

Baltimore theaters were segregated, and separate unions for white and African American projectionists did not merge until 1948. Licensed in 1910, George H. Douglass was among the city's first black projectionists. Refused entry to the white union, Douglass helped form the Colored Motion Picture Operators' Union in 1921, which provided training and placed members in African American theatres. The union was active in many community events and recognized individuals for their social, political, and economic activism. The May 1941 certificate above was presented to Walter Carr, who created the magazine *Nitelifer*, a weekly publication about Baltimore's clubs and bars. Carr also used the publication to comment on issues important to the black community. The May 1940 certificate below was presented to Juanita Jackson Mitchell, a pioneering African American female lawyer, civil rights activist, and daughter of longtime Baltimore NAACP chapter president Lillie Carroll Jackson.

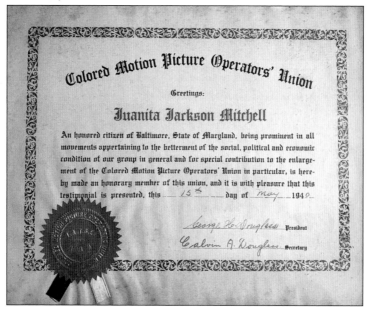

OFFICE:
MADISON 1538

HOME:
MADISON 3625-J

Associated Colored Orchestras
OF BALTIMORE, MD., INC.

L. B. GAMBY
BUSINESS MANAGER
WE FURNISH ACTS
ENTERTAINERS, ETC.

1503 PENNSYLVANIA, AVE,

Littleton B. Gamby worked individually and in partnership with musician Isaiah "Ike" Dixon to promote African American bands. He also owned an important nightclub, Gamby's, in the 1500 block of Pennsylvania Avenue. Gamby also lived within walking distance of his office.

The Baltimore Red Book was published by the National Publicity Bureau in the 1500 block of Pennsylvania Avenue. During the 1930s and 1940s, the *Red Book* attempted to provide a similar service as the *First Colored Directory*, but without the biographical data. J. Gene Payne was a political activist, liquor inspector, entrepreneur, and publisher of the *Red Book*.

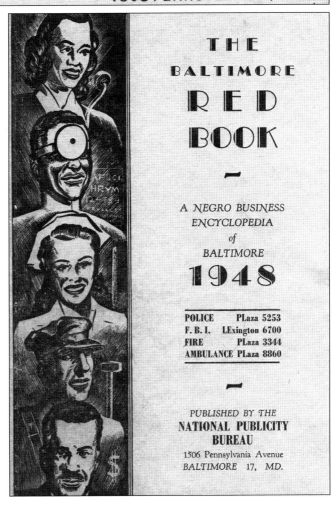

THE
BALTIMORE
RED
BOOK
—

A NEGRO BUSINESS
ENCYCLOPEDIA
of
BALTIMORE
1948

POLICE   PLaza 5253
F. B. I.   LExington 6700
FIRE   PLaza 3344
AMBULANCE PLaza 8860

—

PUBLISHED BY THE
NATIONAL PUBLICITY BUREAU
1506 Pennsylvania Avenue
BALTIMORE 17, MD.

Robert J. Young, standing at center, was a Baltimore booking agent and musician who opened the field for African American musicians to secure engagements to perform in the United States and Europe. Young's Quartet went by other names, including the Jazz Kings. During the 1920s, he toured with Williams and Walker and Will Marion Cook, noted black performers. Cook often stayed in Baltimore at Young's home, the Upton Mansion in the 800 block of West Lanvale Street. Young was also a noted real estate agent. This image was by black photographer Arthur L. Macbeth.

For over 20 years, Arthur Ladlier Macbeth operated a photography studio at three different locations along Pennsylvania Avenue, including one opposite the Douglass Theatre, later renamed the Royal Theatre. Macbeth lived on nearby Pitcher Street, within walking distance of his studios. As a leading black photographer, he documented all aspects of the community. He was a member of the National Negro Business League and the only black life member of the Photographers' Association of America. His body of work spanned Charleston, South Carolina; Norfolk, Virginia; and Baltimore, Maryland. This little girl was one of his photographic subjects.

The public is accustomed to seeing well-dressed and -attired folk in Harlem, but within the confines of Pennsylvania Avenue, the old folks used to say that you were "clean as the board of health." Lucretia Trotter King of Arlington Avenue was clearly going out on the town. The photographer was Penn Studio, in the 900 block of Pennsylvania Avenue, not within the historic district.

Prophet Kiowa Costonie was born Tony Green on an Indian reservation in Utah. After several name changes, he settled on the name Kiowa Costonie and spent a great deal of his life traveling and uplifting the African American community. In 1933, Costonie arrived in Baltimore and organized several boycotts against Pennsylvania Avenue businesses that would not employ black workers. His famous "Buy Where You Can Work" campaign led to the successful hiring of nearly 100 blacks in stores such as Tommy Tucker's Five & Dime and Max Meyers' Shoe Store. Costonie autographed this photograph for his friend P.E. Johnson.

Kenneth Bass, pictured here outside the Club Casino, was a trusted confidant and business partner of entrepreneur and political boss William "Little Willie" Adams. Bass was one of the first two men who Adams trusted to bring into his fledgling numbers-running business. To reward their loyalty, Adams allowed Bass and another associate, Askew Gatewood, to run the Club Casino in the 1500 block of Pennsylvania Avenue, which he opened in 1940.

The Colored Businessmen's Exchange was established around 1912 "to serve the colored businessmen of Baltimore and further their interests by any legitimate means." It was in the 1200 block of Pennsylvania Avenue. William H. Dodd was president, and Joseph S. Fennell, owner of Fennell's Pharmacy on Druid Hill Avenue and Biddle Street, was vice president of the organization. At their first annual banquet in 1916, speakers included Harry S. Cummings, Baltimore's first black city councilman; and Harry T. Pratt, future principal of Douglass High School. To support the organization, African American attorney and funeral home operator William Norman Bishop purchased four tickets with this July 1922 check.

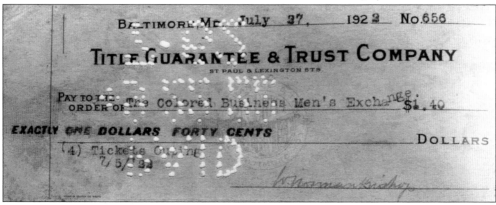

Herman Katkow was the founder and president of the Pennsylvania Avenue Lafayette Market Association (PALMA), a business association formed in the early 1950s to support Pennsylvania Avenue merchants, both African American and white. Katkow and his wife, Ethel, owned and operated the Beverly Dress Shop in the 1700 block of Pennsylvania Avenue, directly across from the Lafayette Market, now known as the Pennsylvania Avenue Market. The association sponsored voter registration drives with Lillie Carroll Jackson and the Baltimore NAACP and also produced the *PALMA News*, a publication with business advertisements and discounts for the community.

Victorine Q. Adams, daughter of Joseph and Estelle Quille and wife of noted entrepreneur William "Little Willie" Adams, was the owner of the Charm Centre, a ladies' apparel shop opened in 1948 in the 1800 block of Pennsylvania Avenue. Victorine was the only woman to serve on the PALMA committee. She also became the first African American woman to serve on the Baltimore City Council. This April 1962 letter on Charm Centre stationery, signed by Victorine, was addressed to a Mr. Cushner, thanking him for serving refreshments at a political event held at Baltimore's historic St. Peter Claver Catholic Church.

BASKETBALL

New Albert Auditorium

Date 2/2/41

Bruins vs. Dolly King's Stars

ISSUED BY Art Carter

THIS PASS and 35 Cents including Tax to be exchanged at Box Office for ticket to game.

Dolly King's All Stars, also known as Dolly King's Stars, were an African American basketball team managed by William "Dolly" King, one of a handful of black players to play in the National Basketball League, the predecessor to the NBA. In February 1941, the Stars played against the Washington Bruins at the New Albert Auditorium in the 1200 block of Pennsylvania Avenue. The Stars won 41-39 in a thrilling game before 800 fans. The ticket is signed by Art Carter, journalist, sports editor, and managing editor of the *Washington Afro-American* newspaper.

1841 PENNSYLVANIA AVENUE
BALTIMORE, MARYLAND

Committee Of Citizens Interested In The Welfare Of The Colored Group

DEAR VOTER:

We take the privilege of calling to your attention a matter of vital importance to the citizens of this Commonwealth. There is being made a desperate effort to elect a Republican Governor, a United States Senator and other State officials. In order to accomplish this task, it is imperative on our part to impress the voters to make every sacrifice to vote intelligently in the Primary Election on September 12th, 1934.

This election is of greater importance to our group than to any other group in the City and State. For instance: we need educational and character-building institutions, the existence of which we are at present denied, notwithstanding numerous unheeded appeals to the authorities in power. For example:

1. An institution for the feeble-minded, which, at the same time, tends to prevent occurrences such as happened in this State some time ago.

2. We need the replacement of Cheltenham with an up to-date institution to care for the 600 unfortunate Negro youths who at the present time are treated inhumanly, with the result that at the expiration of their term of confinement they enter into society without any improvement—provided they live to the end of their imprisonment.

The Committee of Citizens Interested in the Welfare of the Colored Group was established in the 1800 block of Pennsylvania Avenue. The committee informed the African American community about educational, social, political, and economic issues and encouraged residents to exercise their right to vote. Some committee members included Rev. Dr. Ernest Lyon, former US minister to Liberia and pastor of the AME Church within the district; Dr. Howard E. Young, proprietor of Young's Pharmacy on Druid Hill Avenue; Dr. Lillie Carroll Jackson, longtime president of the Baltimore NAACP; Estelle Hall Young of the League of Women Voters; and Willard W. Allen, the worshipful grand master of the Masons and president of Southern Life Insurance Company.

This December 1928 bill from pediatrician Dr. Harry Frances Brown shows that Pennsylvania Avenue was not just about entertainment. Dr. Brown, the father of renowned concert singer Anne Wiggins Brown, had a medical office in the 1900 block of Pennsylvania Avenue, and resided in the 1800 block of Madison Avenue. From 1916 to 1924, Dr. Brown served as the superintendent of Provident Hospital when it was on Biddle Street. Brown was the son of Annie W. Brown, an early well-known female evangelist. His earlier home in the 1500 block of Presstman Street, where his daughter Anne was born in 1912, received landmark designation.

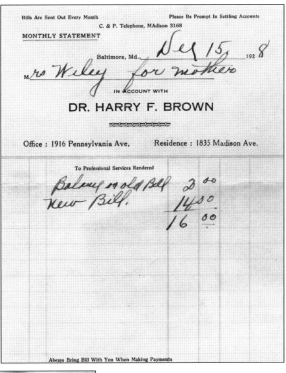

This unidentified woman was a graduate of the Provident Hospital Nursing School. She was photographed at Williams Studio, a black photographer located in the 1500 block of Pennsylvania Avenue.

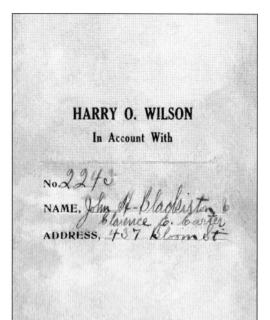

Harry O'Neil Wilson was the son of one of Baltimore's early principals in the segregated school system. Harry O. Wilson founded a bank with several locations in Baltimore, including a branch on Pennsylvania Avenue with limited evening hours. In the midst of the Great Depression in March 1933, Pres. Franklin D. Roosevelt declared a national bank holiday to stave off a run on accounts. However, Wilson was so financially solvent that he was able to pay off every dollar requested by his depositors. He also established Wilson Park, an African American enclave, and was the founder of the Mutual Benefit Society, a life insurance company. Wilson was an active philanthropist in both the black and white communities.

The Universal Negro Improvement Association (UNIA) was founded by political activist and entrepreneur Marcus Garvey in 1914 and had chapters nationwide. In June 1922, African American attorney James Steward Davis filed the incorporation papers for the Baltimore Chapter No. 83 of the UNIA. Liberty Hall, the name used for UNIA meeting halls, was in the 1400 block of Pennsylvania Avenue. This July 1922 UNIA certificate belonged to black attorney William Norman Bishop, a former law partner of Davis, and was signed by the chapter president, James R.L. Diggs, pastor of Trinity Baptist Church. In the 1920s, Baltimore had 3,000 disciples of Marcus Garvey.

Pawnshops were another way for the community to get money. This Depression-era pawn ticket from the North-Western Loan Office in the 1700 block of Pennsylvania Avenue shows that H. Wallace received $3 for a ring. Entertainers and everyday folk used this pawn shop as a way to help them through difficult times. The shop is still in operation.

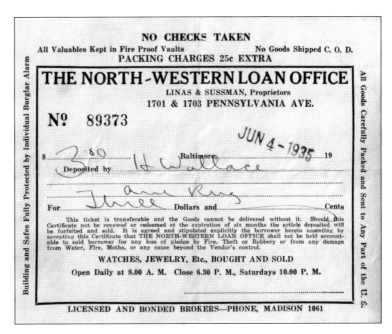

This 1935 ticket was for the Regent Theatre, one of several theaters that catered to African American audiences, located in the 1600 block of Pennsylvania Avenue. The theatre was operated by Louis Hornstein and his sons Simon and Issac, a Jewish family. It was the largest theater on the avenue, with over 2,000 seat, and had its own orchestra. Hornstein only employed blacks and refused to show racist movies. Musicians Cab Calloway, Eubie Blake, and Noble Sissle performed at the Regent. Black heavyweight boxing champion Jack Johnson gave an exhibition at the theater on one of his many visits to Baltimore.

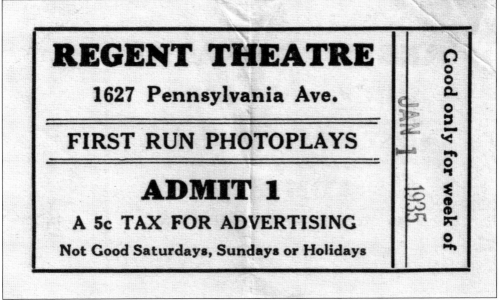

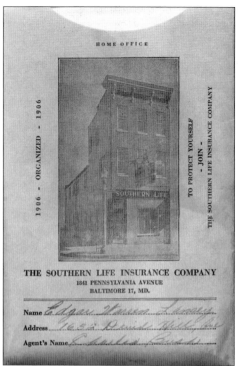

The Southern Life Insurance Company in the 1800 block of Pennsylvania Avenue was established in 1906 as the People's Benefit and Fraternal Society by Rev. Dr. William M. Alexander, civil rights activist and pastor of Baltimore's Sharon Baptist Church. Alexander served as the company's first president. The institution offered sick and death benefits, a safe place for investment, and an avenue of employment for numerous African American men and women. In 1916, the name changed to Southern Life Insurance Company. This insurance packet was for Edgar Warren Lansey of the entrepreneurial Lansey-Williams family, who lived in the 1600 block of Druid Hill Avenue.

This photograph shows the interior of the Southern Life Insurance office. Willard W. Allen, at far right, was a Masonic leader and real estate broker. He became Southern Life's president in 1925. Alfred Nixon, the secretary, is standing beside him. Also pictured are Henrietta H. Jones, a Mrs. Hurtt, and a Mr. Chisum.

Unidentified performers are pictured inside the Avenue Cafe, in the 1500 block of Pennsylvania Avenue. The poster on the wall promotes Pee Wee Wooden's band, which was the popular venue's house band at one time.

Charles P. Tilghman opened the Sphinx Club in 1946 in the 2100 block of Pennsylvania Avenue as a private, members-only club. The club's membership included judges, entertainers, policemen, politicians, doctors, and community leaders. Notable people such as Jackie Robinson, George L. Russell, Big Daddy Lipscomb, and Walter Carr visited the club. Furman L. Templeton, the longtime head of the Baltimore Urban League, developed guidelines for the club's operations and sat on the advisory board. This 1947 membership card belonged to Wilbert O. Dyson, who lived in the 500 block of North Calhoun Street within the district.

Along with souvenir photographs, many clubs offered their guests souvenir matchbooks and drink stirrers. The slogan on the back of this matchbook reads, "Where Old Friends Meet and New Friends Greet."

This August 1958 image shows Charles P. Tilghman, the Sphinx Club's owner, and an unidentified woman in the front of the main club room.

Old Timers Nite was a celebration of the "gay 1890s." Guests wore old-time derby hats, cutaway coats, and button shoes. There were barbershop quartets, giant beer mugs, singing bartenders in checkered vests, and all the men were encouraged to wear handlebar mustaches. This c. 1950s watercolor sketch of Old Timers Nite poked fun at "Doc" Woingust, the club's master of ceremonies, who is depicted holding a stethoscope to the bass, while the club's owner, Charles Tilghman, helps himself to a drink from the instrument.

Three

SEGREGATED EDUCATION

This c. 1950s vernacular image shows an unidentified class, all bundled up in their winter coats and posed in front of one of the most important school buildings in the community, Henry Highland Garnet Elementary School No. 103, on Division and Lanvale Streets. Built in 1877, the school only served white students until 1910, when the building was first used for African American students. In March 1911, it was designated School No. 103, and in 1919, it was renamed in honor of abolitionist Henry Highland Garnet. The bronze tablet at left, which bore the school's new name, was also dedicated in 1919. The unveiling of the tablet was held at nearby Bethel AME Church. Garnet's great-granddaughter was present, as was future Supreme Court justice Thurgood Marshall, who was a student at the time.

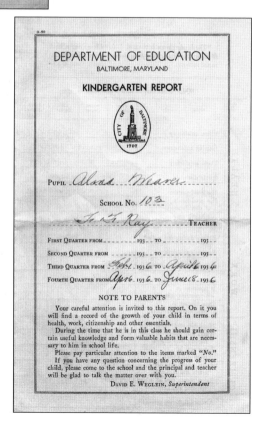

This 1914 assignment for Justine Neal emphasized the importance of penmanship for students, even in elementary school. The Zaner-Bloser style of cursive writing was used in the segregated school system and taught to teachers at the nearby Colored Training School, now Coppin State University. Neal would have been in the first class to attend School No. 103. The Neal family lived on Division Street, within walking distance of the school.

Artifacts from colored schools before *Brown v. Board of Education of Topeka, Kansas* are difficult to find, particularly homework assignments, textbooks, professional and vernacular photographs, and report cards. This Depression-era report card from 1936 was Alma Weaver's, who lived with her family on Druid Hill Avenue, within walking distance of School No. 103.

This c. 1950s photograph shows students and faculty playing outside of School No. 103, promoting physical activity and cleanliness within the community. The words on the trash can read, "Less Dirt, Less Disease, Filth is an Archenemy to Health."

William M. Alexander School No. 112, at Laurens and Calhoun Streets, opened in October 1921. It was named after nearby Sharon Baptist Church's founder and first pastor, Rev. Dr. William M. Alexander. This exterior c. 1930s photograph was taken in the winter, as evidenced by the snow on the ground and the three children bundled up in their winter coats. One of the school's early important principals was George B. Murphy Sr., son of the *Afro-American* newspaper founder.

Baltimore's Colored School System not only produced great students, but also great student-run newspapers. This March 1952 edition of *The William Alexander Times* is one such example. This rare school newspaper was filled with classroom news, poetry, information about speakers, and community updates. The author's mother, Betty Jackson Merrill, and uncle Martin Jackson attended School No. 112.

Similar to nearby School No. 103, Booker T. Washington Junior High School No. 130, at the corner of McCulloh and Lafayette Streets, was originally erected in 1895 as Western Female High School, which was for white students only. In 1929, it received its current name after School No. 106 in South Baltimore gave up the name. Many Baltimore churches and schools were originally built for the white community in the late 1800s, and with increased African American migration, they became black schools and churches to accommodate the growing population.

This 1937 class photograph of School No. 130 features Ellis Larkins (first row, sixth from left), a child piano prodigy who made his debut with the Baltimore City Colored Orchestra at the age of 11. He also played for First Lady Eleanor Roosevelt during her visit to Baltimore. Larkins was the first African American to attend the Peabody Institute of Baltimore, which once barred African Americans. Principal William Anderson (second row, ninth from left) was a graduate of the Colored High School and a longtime principal of School No. 130. Other members of the 1937 class included Louise Sessoms (fourth row, far right), daughter of the Sess' Restaurant owners; William "Billy" Young (first row, ninth from left), child star of the 1937 film *Children of Circumstance*; Mabel Gee Stokes (second row, eleventh from left), longtime educator and president of the Sunday School and Baptist Training Union Convention of Maryland; James "Biddy" Wood (first row, third from left), son of Francis M. Wood, the first director of Baltimore Colored Schools; and Spencer Dobson (fifth row, far right), brother of future pastor of Union Baptist Church Rev. Vernon Dobson.

Months before the United States entered World War II, School No. 130 Evening School had a commencement for its adult students, many of whom worked during the day but wanted to complete their education. Clarence I. Wing was the principal of the evening school, and the commencement speaker was Furman L. Templeton, director of the Baltimore Urban League and respected community activist. A majority of the March 1941 graduates were women.

This rare December 1942 edition of the *Booker T. Bulletin* was the first issue. It honors the school's late principal, William Anderson, and the school's namesake, the formerly enslaved Booker T. Washington, an educator and author who frequently visited Baltimore. Oliver Fitzhugh Oldham was the paper's editor-in-chief. Like other school newspapers, it was filled with classroom and community news, information about guest speakers, poetry, and much more.

Ossarew Fiske Gee III's graduation certificate is pictured here. His parents both attended Booker T. Washington Junior High School. This type of legacy was prominent throughout the colored school system. Gee and his fellow classmates endured the 1968 riots after the death of Dr. Martin Luther King Jr.

Booker T. Washington Junior High School

BALTIMORE CITY PUBLIC SCHOOLS, BALTIMORE, MARYLAND

By Authority of the Board of School Commissioners this

Certificate

has been awarded to

Ossareu F. Gee

in Testimony of the Completion of the course of Study Prescribed for the Ninth Grade

Regular Curriculum

James R. Hite
PRINCIPAL

June 19 19 68

Francis D. Murnaghan
PRESIDENT OF BOARD OF SCHOOL COMMISSIONERS

M. Thomas Goedeke
ASSOCIATE SUPERINTENDENT-IN-CHARGE

In the colored school system, music and art was an integral part of education. For some students, like the ones from Druid Junior High School No. 137 at Clifton Avenue and Francis Street, their first introduction to the arts was in the classroom. These students were likely practicing for a performance because the words "Seating Arrangement" were written on the chalkboard.

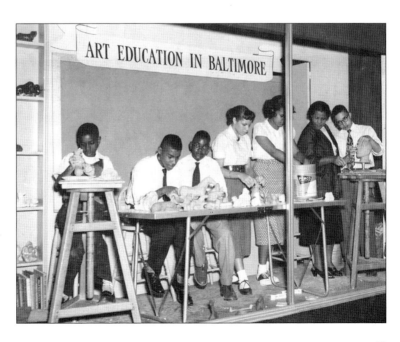

Ethel A. Clarke, art teacher at School No. 137, and her students demonstrate sculpting in the show window at Hochschild, Kohn & Company in 1953. The demonstration was a part of the International Art Exchange Project of the American Red Cross.

John H. Murphy Elementary School No. 119 was at Gilmor and Mosher Streets. This 1939 image of a classroom Nativity play was photographed by Claiborne's Studio. Note how the young ladies were focused on the play, but the young boys were focused on the camera. The principal was William T. Griggs. The school was named for John H. Murphy Sr., founder of the *Afro-American* newspaper.

John Hurst Elementary School No. 120, named for African Methodist Episcopal bishop John Hurst, was at Pennsylvania Avenue and Robert Street. Florence Gloster, sitting in the front row, was the principal. Edgar Warren Lansey is seated next to her. The honor students for the class were Ben Mason, Barbara Wilson, Ruth Tate, Veronica Shipley, Cynthia Gillis, Verna Mitchell, Delores Massenburg, and Priscilla Butler.

Colored High and Training School, Baltimore, Md.

The Colored High and Training School was established in 1883 in the old city hall, now the Peale Center for Baltimore History and Architecture. In 1901, the school moved to the location on this postcard, Pennsylvania Avenue and Dolphin Street, where it remained until 1924, when it moved to its newly built school on Carey, Calhoun, and Baker Streets. Some of the graduates from this location included Baltimore NAACP president Lillie Carroll Jackson; educator, musician, and Arctic explorer Herbert M. Frisby; actor Clarence Muse; actor Avon Long; educator and suffragette Lucy Diggs Slowe; and educator and YMCA leader William H.J. Beckett. This postcard was produced by African American pharmacist Joseph S. Fennell, proprietor of Fennell's Pharmacy.

It is extremely difficult to uncover early Colored High School photographs. This fragment is part of a broken panoramic photo of the class of 1923. Members of the June 1923 graduating class included Harry S. Cummings Jr., son of 1880s pioneering African American Baltimore City councilman Harry S. Cummings; George B. Murphy Jr., son of respected principal George B. Murphy Sr.; and Leon S. Roye, pioneering principal of the Havre de Grace Colored School in Havre de Grace, Maryland. The 1923 class had triplets who graduated at the top of their class: Miles Wise, valedictorian; Ethel Wise, salutatorian; and Llewellyn Wise, third in the class.

This one page, salvaged from a scrapbook, shows some stylish women from Douglass High School's 1924 class displaying the fashions of the day. Justine T. Neal is on the bottom row, second from the left. Her classmates are unidentified.

The high schools had February and June graduations, including this February 1930 graduating class at Douglass High. This was at the Carey, Calhoun, and Baker Streets location. Alfred W. Walker (fourth row, far left), was the valedictorian and son of Rev. William W. Walker, pastor of Madison Avenue Presbyterian Church.

When William H. Smith, June 1939 graduate of Douglass High, was caught doodling, he was instructed to paint a series of murals on the high school walls. This one depicts formerly enslaved abolitionist and author Frederick Douglass and Pres. Abraham Lincoln holding a document that reads "Emancipation."

Mr. and Mrs. Herbert M. Frisby at home to the
Graduates and Faculty of Nineteen Hundred Thirty-six
of the Douglass Evening High School
Sunday Afternoon, May thirty-first
Nineteen Hundred Thirty-six
Four to Six o'oclock

1806 Druid Hill Avenue
Baltimore, Maryland

Herbert M. Frisby graduated from the Colored High School when it was at the corner of Pennsylvania Avenue and Dolphin Street. Frisby taught at Coppin State Teachers College, now Coppin State University. In 1936, he was the principal of the Douglass Evening High School. This invitation was extended to the high school's 1936 graduates and faculty to attend a reception at his home in the 1800 block of Druid Hill Avenue.

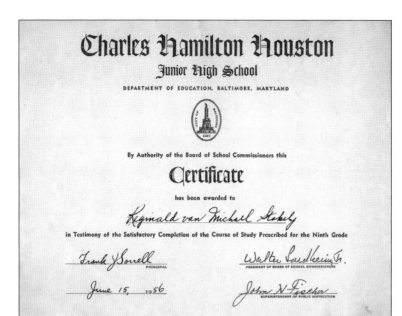

Charles Hamilton Houston

Junior High School

DEPARTMENT OF EDUCATION, BALTIMORE, MARYLAND

By Authority of the Board of School Commissioners this

Certificate

has been awarded to

Reginald van Michael Stokely

in Testimony of the Satisfactory Completion of the Course of Study Prescribed for the Ninth Grade

Frank J Sorrell
PRINCIPAL

Walter Sondheim Jr.
PRESIDENT OF BOARD OF SCHOOL COMMISSIONERS

June 15, 1956

John N Fischer
SUPERINTENDENT OF PUBLIC INSTRUCTION

In the early 1950s, School No. 181 was named Charles Hamilton Houston in honor of lawyer and dean of the Howard University School of Law in Washington, DC. Longtime educator Frank Sorrell was the principal. The school was at Carey, Calhoun, and Baker Streets, the former location of Douglass High School before it moved to Gwynn Falls Parkway.

George Washington Carver Vocational Technical School opened in 1925 and was named in honor of the inventor and Tuskegee University faculty member. Originally created to provide training for boys, the school eventually widened its enrollment to include girls. At Carver, students learned trades in carpentry, tailoring, auto mechanics, plumbing, engineering, and cosmetology. The school was in Lafayette Square, at the corner of Carrollton and Lafayette Avenues.

This March 1952 letter encouraged parents to attend an upcoming Parent-Teacher Association meeting at Carver. The names of teachers are listed in the letter.

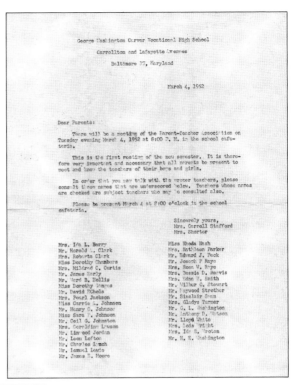

George Washington Carver Vocational High School

Carrollton and Lafayette Avenues

Baltimore 17, Maryland

March 4, 1952

Dear Parents:

There will be a meeting of the Parent-Teacher Association on Tuesday evening March 4, 1952 at 8:00 P. M. in the school cafeteria.

This is the first meeting of the new semester. It is therefore very important and necessary that all parents be present to meet and know the teachers of their boys and girls.

In order that you may talk with the proper teachers, please consult those names that are underscored below. Teachers whose names are checked are subject teachers who may be consulted also.

Please be present March 4 at 8:00 o'clock in the school cafeteria.

Sincerely yours,
Mrs. Carroll Stafford
Mrs. Shorter

Mrs. Ida L. Berry
Mr. Harold L. Clark
Mrs. Roberta Clark
Miss Dorothy Chambers
Mrs. Mildred C. Curtis
Mr. James Early
Mr. Herd B. Hollis
Miss Dorothy Jones
Mr. David Nichols
Mrs. Pearl Jackson
Miss Carrie A. Johnson
Mr. Henry C. Johnson
Miss Sara P. Johnson
Mr. Ceil G. Johnston
Mrs. Geraldine Lawson
Mr. Linwood Jordan
Mr. Leon Lofton
Mr. Charles Lynch
Mr. Lemuel Lewis
Mr. James T. Moore

Miss Rhoda Nash
Mrs. Kathleen Parker
Mr. Edward J. Peck
Mr. Joseph P. Raye
Mrs. Rosa W. Raye
Mrs. Bessie D. Reavis
Mrs. Edna N. Smith
Mr. Wilbur O. Stewart
Mr. Haywood Strother
Mr. Sinclair Swan
Mrs. Gladys Turner
Mr. G. L. Washington
Mr. Anthony D. Watson
Mr. Lloyd White
Mrs. Ida Wright
Mrs. Ida E. Wroton
Mr. H. R. Washington

Robert Moses Hicks, known as the "Lafayette Square Governor" and "Happy Days," was a beloved figure to the Carver students. For 18 years, Hicks stood on the corner of Lafayette and Carrollton Avenues, sold confectionery, and encouraged the students to stay in school. When Hicks retired in 1952 at the age of 71, the students and faculty honored him for his years of uplift and dedication to the thousands of students who crossed his path. Hicks lived in the 500 block of Carrollton Avenue. In this photograph by Arthur L. Macbeth, Hicks is on the right.

The Baltimore Institute of Musical Arts (BIMA) was incorporated in 1943 by Robert P. Iula, a composer, conductor, and municipal music executive, along with Evelyn Deshiell Ebert and Dr. John Leslie Jones. They established BIMA as an alternative to the Peabody Institute, which did not admit African American students. The institute offered music training and was originally housed in Dr. Jones's home in the 1100 block of Myrtle Avenue before it moved to the 800 block of West Lanvale Street. The school had a fully integrated faculty, which included many musicians from the Baltimore Symphony Orchestra. It was endorsed by many prominent black Baltimoreans, including Willard W. Allen, Sarah F. Diggs, George Douglass, and the Baltimore NAACP.

 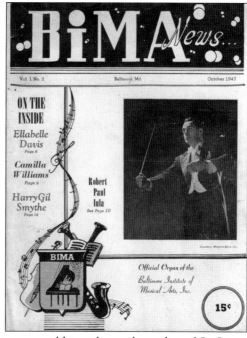

Dr. Jones, a chiropractor, was a World War I veteran, world traveler, and member of St. James Episcopal Church. The school published its own magazine, *BIMA News*, from 1947 to 1949.

The Baltimore Branch of the Cortez W. Peters Business School was co-founded in 1935 by Cortez W. Peters, the all-time world speed champion typist, and future city councilman Walter T. Dixon, who served as the dean. Originally established in the 2000 block of Druid Hill Avenue, it eventually moved to the 1200 block of Pennsylvania Avenue due to its rapid growth. There was another location in the 500 block of Gold Street. The school trained African Americans for clerical and professional work and offered courses in shorthand, accounting, commercial law, and journalism. According to one of its bulletins, it was considered one of "America's finest privately owned Negro schools." In this 1938 graduating class photograph, Walter Dixon is in the middle of the first row. Instructor Evelyn Wilkey, noted for her disciplinary style, is seated on his left.

This Cortez W. Peters 1942 graduating class was photographed by noted African American photographer Paul Henderson. In the first row, sixth from left, is Olivia "Chinky" Pierce, who later married Walter T. Dixon. She was widely known by the politically incorrect nickname because of her slanted eyes.

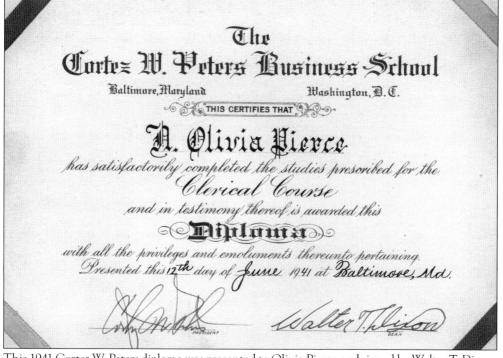

This 1941 Cortez W. Peters diploma was presented to Olivia Pierce and signed by Walter T. Dixon.

This Cortez W. Peters classroom activity was captured by Brown's Studio, in the 1400 block of Pennsylvania Avenue. Walter Dixon is standing to the right, overseeing the typing lessons in the school at the 1200 block of Pennsylvania Avenue. One sign on the wall reads, "When your wrist pains, your practice is doing you good," which was meant to encourage the students to practice their typing skills. The other sign reads, "Release your keys as soon as they have printed."

9. Aubrey Bodine

This c. 1950s photograph of Walter T. Dixon was captured by A. Aubrey Bodine, a *Baltimore Sun* photographer for over 50 years who was regarded as one of the finest photographers of the 20th century. His pictures were exhibited in hundreds of shows and museums, and he won many awards. Bodine's work was also featured in numerous books, magazines, calendars, and murals.

Four

SACRED SITES OF WORSHIP

Sharp Street Memorial United Methodist Church, formerly known as Sharp Street Memorial Methodist Church and Sharp Street Methodist Episcopal Church, was established in 1802. In 1898, the church purchased a lot on the corner of Dolphin and Etting Streets and erected a new structure, pictured here, during the pastorate of Dr. Daniel W. Hayes. Early pastors of Sharp Street were Rev. Alfred Young, formerly enslaved on Maryland's Eastern Shore; Rev. John A. Holmes; Bishop W.A.C. Hughes Sr.; and Rev. McHenry J. Naylor. Lillie Carroll Jackson was the first chairwoman of the church's trustee board.

This fragment of a much larger c. 1910 image shows, from left to right seated in the first row, formerly enslaved William H.D.T. Wilson, a member of US Colored Troop Company B, 39th Regiment; Rev. S.R. Hughes, son of a formerly enslaved minister from Carroll County, Maryland; and Hughes's son, future bishop W.A.C. Hughes Sr., who pastored Sharp Street Church from 1905 to 1912. Rev. Daniel W. Hayes, standing third from right in the second row, was responsible for moving the church from South Baltimore to its current location at Dolphin and Etting Streets. The other men are unidentified.

Sharp Street Church's Boy Scout Troop No. 275 was organized in 1928 under the leadership of scoutmaster Oscar Simmons, with Levi Jolley and Leroy Coles as assistants. This photograph of the troop a year or two after its inception shows Milton Edward Stanley (first row, far right), a future Baltimore school principal; and Eugene Prettyman (second row, fourth from right), a musician, educator, and high ranking Boy Scout leader.

This Sharp Street Memorial Methodist Church 140th anniversary booklet from 1942 is loaded with important church and community history that highlights the church's role in the community.

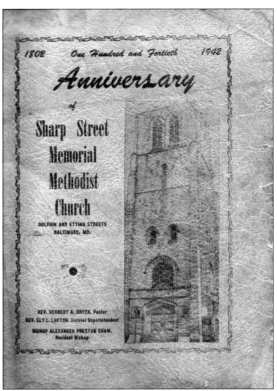

Rev. Dr. Harvey E. Johnson, minister and pioneering civil rights leader, was born enslaved in Fauquier County, Virginia. In 1872, Johnson became the fifth pastor of Union Baptist Church in the 1200 block of Druid Hill Avenue, where he remained for 50 years. During his tenure, he expanded the membership from 200 to over 2,000. Johnson's administration led to the creation of at least 13 other churches and produced at least 14 impactful ministers. Johnson was the founder of the Mutual United Brotherhood of Liberty, a precursor to the NAACP.

Amelia Etta Hall Johnson, wife of Rev. Dr. Harvey Johnson, was a noted author and educator. She wrote novels, short fiction, and poetry under the name Mrs. A.E. Johnson. Much of her work, which has been compared to that of Paul Laurence Dunbar, focused on the social circumstances of her characters, rather than their racial or ethnic aspects. She edited many of her husband's writings. Attorney and civil rights activist W. Ashbie Hawkins stated that she "attributed much to her husband's career."

African American photographer Early G. Lane captured the 1925 unveiling of the monument to Rev. Dr. Harvey Johnson. Rev. David E. Over, pastor of the church at the time and the one responsible for Johnson's monument, is at left directly behind it. Johnson's lifetime friend and mentor, formerly enslaved pastor Rev. Dr. Walter H. Brooks of Nineteenth Street Baptist Church in Washington, DC, is also behind the monument, second from right. Rev. Dr. George F. Bragg, publisher, author, educator, and pastor of St. James Episcopal Church, is behind the monument at far right. When the National Negro Bar Association held its annual conference in Baltimore that year, members laid a wreath at Johnson's monument.

Rev. Vernon N. Dobson became the pastor of Union Baptist Church in 1967 and served for almost 40 years. His civil rights "Goon Squad" included Congressman Parren J. Mitchell, Rev. Marion Bascom, Rev. Wendell Phillips, Judge Joseph Howard Sr., and Lalit Gadhia, amongst others. Reverend Dobson graduated from Douglass High School and Howard University in Washington, DC. Dobson is pictured here at home (second row, second from left) with his wife, Napoleon, on his right, and surrounded by his children.

Bethel African Methodist Episcopal Church was founded in 1785 by Rev. Daniel Coker, a presiding elder in the AME conference. Rev. Dr. Daniel Grafton Hill Sr. successfully relocated the church from Lafayette Avenue to its current location in the 1300 block of Druid Hill Avenue in 1910. Reverend Hill (third row, seventh from left) is pictured here with a group of parishioners, possibly at Druid Hill Park. Throughout the years, the church was open for many community events, like graduations, dedications, and prominent speakers. Hill and his family lived in the 400 block of Mosher Street; he could walk to and from his beloved church. Hill and his wife, Margaret Peck, had 10 children, including Violet Hill Whyte, the first African American woman to be appointed to the Baltimore City police in 1937, and Grace Hill Jacobs, dean of instruction at Coppin State College, now University.

This 1924 photograph shows the women of Bethel AME's executive board parent body. From left to right are Annie M. Wortham, Clara E. Harris, Bertha Hurst, Mary S.C. Beckett, Lydia Stewart, Lucille D. Mumford, Mary F. Handy, Emma W. Johnson, Christina S. Smith, Jennie M. Palmer, Dovie K. Clarke, Jennie M. Hunter, Sadie J. Anderson, Hattie L. Shelton, and Emily C. Kinch. The child seated at front was the group's mascot. Bertha Hurst and Mary Handy were the wives of two AME bishops, John Hurst and James A. Handy.

Bethel AME's Senior Missionary Society is pictured with future bishop Harrison J. Bryant (front row, center). His wife, Edith H. Bryant, on his right, was president of the society. Bryant pastored Bethel for 16 years, and in 1964 was the 13th pastor to become a bishop. His son John R. Bryant pastored Bethel for 13 years and also became a bishop.

Payne Memorial AME Church was founded in 1897 and named for Daniel A. Payne, the sixth AME bishop. This October 1947 certificate honors Annie M. Sanders for her 30 years of service to the church. At this time, the church was in the 400 block of Laurens Street, and Rev. C. Baker Pearle was the pastor.

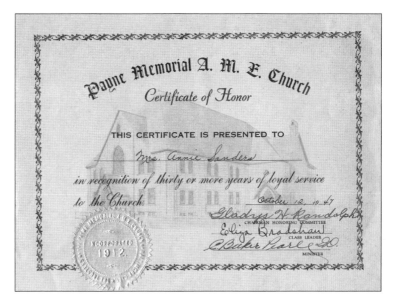

This November 1950 photograph shows Rev. W.P. Mitchell, who pastored Payne for over 30 years and was the church's longest-serving pastor. The little girl is JoAnn Collier Black. The church was under reconstruction at the time.

This photograph shows the burial of longtime Payne AME Church member Laura Virginia Gilles, who died in August 1954. Rev. W.P. Mitchell is standing at the casket at left.

ANNIVERSARY CELEBRATION

TRINITY BAPTIST CHURCH

DRUID HILL AVENUE & McMECHEN STREET BALTIMORE, Md.

Trinity Baptist Church, at the corner of Druid Hill Avenue and McMechen Street, was founded in 1888 by Dr. Garnett R. Waller, Rev. Daniel K. Creigler, Martha Parks, Alexander and Sarah Rieh, and Savannah Goldman. Waller was one of the founders of the Niagara Movement, a precursor to the NAACP. Entrepreneur Harry O. Wilson, who was related to Waller by marriage, was a major financial contributor to the church and served on several committees. This anniversary celebration pamphlet was printed by Clarke Press, in the 2100 block of Druid Hill Avenue.

"Blessed are the dead which die in the Lord, from henceforth, Yea, saith the Spirit, that they may rest from their labors; and their works do follow them."—REV. 14:13.

1923 Tenth Anniversary Memorial 1933
——FOR THE LATE——
Rev. Jas. R. L. Diggs, A. B., A. M., Ph. D.

Former Pastor of Trinity Baptist Church, Baltimore, Maryland

SUNDAY MAY 28, 1933 AT 3 P. M.

(Please give ten cents for each year.)

NAME .... *Clarence Orr* .... AMOUNT *50*

REV. V. V. K. STOKES, Pastor.   W. H. JACKSON, Church Clerk

Rev. James Robert Lincoln Diggs succeeded Reverend Waller as Trinity's pastor in 1915. Like Waller, Diggs was one of the founders of the Niagara Movement. In 1918, he also established the Baltimore chapter of the UNIA, whose founder Marcus Garvey spoke at the church in 1922. In May 1920, Diggs moved the congregation from its former site at Charles and Twentieth Streets to the current location at the corner of Druid Hill Avenue and McMechen Street. This 1933 memorial offering envelope belonged to Clarence Orr, a longtime Trinity member who donated 50¢ honoring Diggs, who had been deceased for 10 years.

Rev. Volley V.K. Stokes pastored Trinity for more than 30 years. He lived in the 1500 block of McCulloh Street.

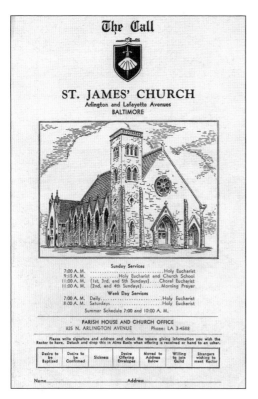

Founded in 1824, St. James Episcopal Church is the nation's second-oldest African Episcopal congregation.

In 1932, Rev. Dr. George Freeman Bragg moved the church to its current location at Arlington and Lafayette Avenues. Bragg pastored St. James for over 40 years and was a publisher, author, and educator. This 1920s Christmas card is addressed to African American attorney William N. Bishop and signed by Bragg.

Rev. Tollie L. Caution is listed as a ministerial son of Rev. Bragg in *History of the Afro-American Group of the Episcopal Church*, published in 1922. Arthur L. Macbeth captured this image of Caution.

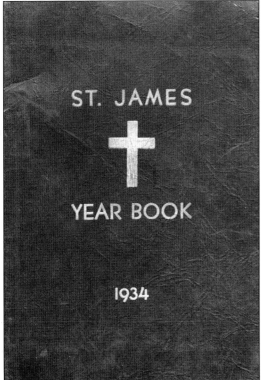

This 1934 *St. James Year Book* was the first one the church produced. The editor was John Leslie Jones, World War I veteran and founder of the Baltimore Institute of Musical Arts. The yearbook documented church history, clubs, organizations, and community businesses.

In 1891, Fr. Charles Randolph Uncles became the fourth African American to be ordained a Roman Catholic priest and the first to be ordained on American soil. Uncles was a professor at the now-defunct Epiphany College in Walbrook Junction. He was an assistant pastor of St. Peter Claver Catholic Church, the second-oldest African American Roman Catholic Church in the nation, during the summers of 1893, 1894, and 1896. Arthur Macbeth captured this image of Uncles.

St. Peter Claver Catholic Church also had a school, as evidenced by this March 1945 image of a fifth-grade class. The nuns were no-nonsense educators and strict disciplinarians. Note the poses and clothing of each of the children.

YOU ARE CORDIALLY INVITED TO ATTEND

A RECEPTION

Given In Honor Of

REV. D. E. RICE

AT ST. JOHN A. M. E. CHURCH

N. Carrollton Ave. nr. Lanyale St.

Tuesday Evening, July 31st, 1934, at 8 P. M.

ADMISSION - - 25 CENTS

Mrs. Bertha Waters, Chr.   Mrs. Lillie Johuson, Sect.

Rev. D. E. Rice, Pastor

This 1934 ticket was for a reception in honor of Rev. D.E. Rice, pastor of St. John. In 1929, Rice moved the congregation to its current site on Carrollton Avenue. The new church building was dedicated by Bishop A.L. Gaines. During the Depression, the church frequently had fundraising events to support its congregational needs.

Before he was consecrated a bishop, A.L. Gaines was connected to various AME churches in Baltimore, including Bethel and St. John. His wife, Minnie L. Gaines, was a member of the Women's Suffrage League and the elite DuBois Circle, an auxiliary of the Niagara Movement.

Metropolitan United Methodist Church moved to its current location at the corner of Carrollton and Lafayette Avenues in 1928 under the pastorate of Rev. Ernest S. Williams. He was succeeded the following year by Rev. Charles Young Trigg, pictured here. Trigg was also president of the Baltimore NAACP from about 1933 to 1935, when Lillie Carroll Jackson assumed the role.

REV. CHARLES YOUNG TRIGG, D. D.
PASTOR, METROPOLITAN METHODIST CHURCH
BALTIMORE, MARYLAND

GOSPEL CRUSADE
HAMILTON METHODIST CHURCH
LOS ANGELES, CALIFORNIA
OCTOBER, 1939

This 1937 Metropolitan Methodist Episcopal Church ticket is an example of the church providing its own fundraising and community fellowship.

A MUSICAL AND LITERARY PROGRAM

GIVEN BY   CLASS NO. 4
AT METROPOLITAN M. E. CHURCH
LANVALE STREET AT CARROLLTON AVE

on Monday December 6th, 1937   At 8:30 p. m.
IN THE SOCIAL HALL

ADMISSION   -   10 CENTS

REFRESHMENTS ON SALE
Mrs. Lucille, Dean, Chairman   Mr. John C. Dyson, Leader
REV. CHARLES Y. TRIGG, PASTOR

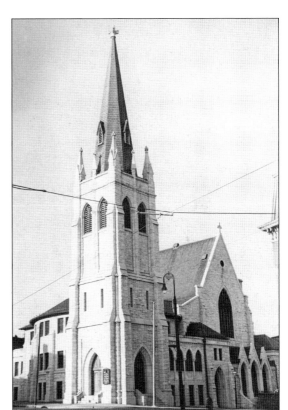

Macedonia Baptist Church was established in 1874 as a product of Union Baptist Church. In 1925, the congregation moved to its current site at the corner of Lafayette and Fremont Avenues. Some prominent pastors include Rev. A.B. Callis, Rev. D.G. Mack, and Rev. Dr. Williard L. Clayton.

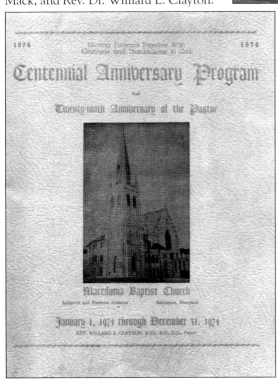

In 1885, Rev. William M. Alexander and nine members of Macedonia Baptist Church created Sharon Baptist Church. Alexander was a member of the Mutual United Brotherhood of Liberty, a civil rights organization that was a precursor to the NAACP. He also established Southern Life Insurance Company in the 1800 block of Pennsylvania Avenue. Reverend Alexander encouraged the establishment of the Northwestern Supply Company and inspired his parishioners to rent stalls in Lafayette Market for the sale of vegetables, fruits, and meat.

This real-photo postcard shows the second location of Sharon Baptist Church on Calhoun and Laurens Streets, from 1885 to 1900. Its current location on Stricker and Presstman Streets was purchased in 1914.

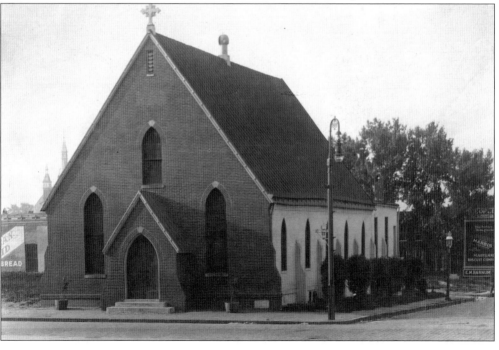

As the fourth pastor of Sharon Baptist Church, Rev. Dr. Alfred C.D. Vaughn has led the congregation for over 30 years, since 1986, and is presently the senior pastor. This photograph was taken around the 1980s.

Unity Christian Church, now known as Unity United Methodist Church, was established in 1929 and is at the corner of Stricker Street and Edmondson Avenue. Within the neighborhood was the Harlem Theatre on Gilmor Street and the Club Astoria on Edmondson Avenue.

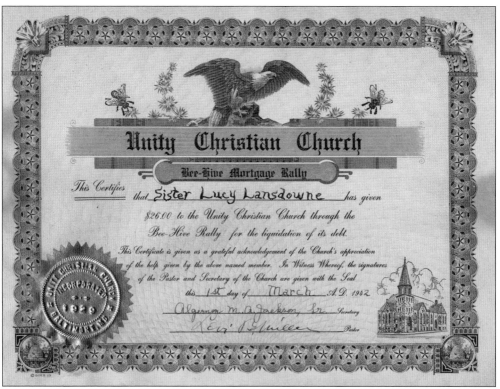

This March 1942 certificate acknowledges that member Lucy Lansdowne donated $26 to liquidate Unity Christian Church's debt. It was signed by the church's pastor, Rev. Levi B. Miller.

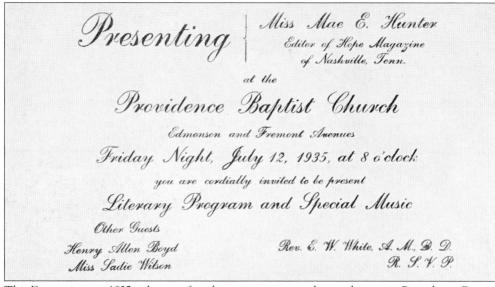

This Depression-era 1935 ticket was for a literary program and special music at Providence Baptist Church featuring Mae E. Hunter, editor of *Hope Magazine* of Nashville, Tennessee. Hunter was also a member of the National Baptist Convention. The other speaker was Henry Allen Boyd, founder of the *Nashville Globe*. At the time, the church was in the 800 block of Edmondson Avenue, and Rev. Eugene W. White was the pastor.

Annual Church Conference

• 1 9 5 5 •

• 1 9 5 5 •

PROVIDENCE BAPTIST CHURCH

FRIDAY, JANUARY 14, 1955

M. G. WOOD, *Minister*   E. DeSHIELDS, *Secretary*

Rev. Marcus Garvey Wood came to Providence Baptist Church in 1952 and pastored for 53 years. He earned his master of divinity degree from Crozer Theological Seminary in Pennsylvania, where one of his classmates and friends was the Rev. Dr. Martin Luther King Jr. This friendship led to Wood's involvement in the 1960s civil rights movement. In 1981, he moved the congregation to its current site in the 1400 block of Pennsylvania Avenue.

1
July 25th, 1949.

The Deacon Board of the madison Ave, Presbyterian church, met at the church on the above date at 8:30 P.m. Monday. Meeting called to order and opened with prayer by Rev. R. J. Daniels. Deacons present were messers. Wm. J. Berry, M. Britt, R. J. Carpenter sr, H. Cummings, P. Daniels, C. H. Jenkins, Edwin Johnson, L. Johnson, and F. L. Templeton.

Rev. Daniels explained, the meeting had been called, in order to get the Deacons organized, and a program started.

In the absence of a constitution, it was moved, seconded and passed that we proceed with the election of a chairman, Co-chairman, Secretary and a Treasurer.

The following officers were elected unanimously:-

Furman L. Templeton — chairman.
C. Henry Jenkins — Co-Chairman.
Raymond J Carpenter — Secretary.
William J. Berry — Treasurer.

It was then decided by the body to have the following committees appointed
(1)- visiting (sick).
(2)- membership. (Delinquent and new).
(1)- Sick committee was as follows:-
L. Johnson, P. Daniels + Wm. Berry + M. Britt.
(2)- Delinquent and new members - were as follows; C. Henry Jenkins, A. Kelly, J. Nicholas and Edwin Johnson.

Madison Street Presbyterian Church was established in 1848 and moved to Madison Street in 1850. In 1948, the name changed to Madison Avenue Presbyterian Church. Nine of the church's influential pastors were graduates of Lincoln University of Pennsylvania, the nation's first African American degree-granting institution. This July 1949 page from a deacon's board ledger shows the prominent members of the church, including Furman L. Templeton and Harry S. Cummings Jr. Rev. Reginald J. Daniels was the pastor.

As a result of his landmark civil rights case *Murray v. Pearson* in 1935, Donald Gaines Murray was the first African American to enter the University of Maryland School of Law since 1890. Future Supreme Court justice and native Baltimorean Thurgood Marshall and his mentor, Charles Hamilton Houston, were Murray's attorneys. Murray was raised by his maternal grandparents, Bishop A.L. Gaines and his wife, Minnie, in the 1500 block of McCulloh Street. He served in World War II, and upon his return to Maryland worked on many NAACP legal cases. He was a longtime member of Madison Avenue Presbyterian Church.

Service of Triumph

for

Donald Gaines Murray
May 24, 1913 — April 7, 1986

Thursday, April 10, 1986
Family Hour: 11:30 A.M. — Funeral: 12:00 Noon

Madison Avenue Presbyterian Church
2106 Madison Avenue
Baltimore, Maryland

REV. HERSCHEL MARTIN, *Interim Preacher*
REV. REGINALD DANIELS, *Pastor Emeritus*

Five

FIGHTING FOR THE CAUSE

Rev. Dr. William Abraham Creditt, son of Union Baptist Church founder Rev. Dr. Harvey Johnson, was a general agent for the civil rights organization Mutual United Brotherhood of Liberty. The Creditt family was very involved in real estate, medicine, education, religion, and activism. William's mother, Mary L. Creditt, took over her husband's business when he died and owned substantial property; William's brother Daniel was a principal in the segregated school system; and another brother, James, was a medical doctor. William was the great uncle of musician Cab Calloway. This photograph was taken by noted African American photographer Addison Scurlock.

Rev. John Alexander Holmes was the pastor of Metropolitan United Methodist Church for over 19 years. He was also president of the Colored Law and Order League, established in 1906, a group of African American ministers, lawyers, doctors, educators, and business leaders who conducted a study of predominantly white-owned saloons and their proximity to colored schools. The group presented its findings to the Colored Ministerial Union in hopes of improving the poor conditions in black neighborhoods. Holmes's son Dr. Dwight O.W. Holmes was the first black president of Morgan State University.

Lucy Diggs Slowe was the first student from the Colored High School, on the corner of Pennsylvania Avenue and Dolphin Street, to receive a scholarship to Howard University, in 1904. Upon her graduation in 1908, she returned to the Colored High School to teach for several years. Slowe spoke regularly on women's rights and suffrage and was one of the original nine founders of the Alpha Kappa Alpha sorority. In 1917, she became the first African American woman to win a major sports title when she won the American Tennis Association's first tournament. In 1922, she was appointed the first dean of women at her alma mater, Howard University. Slowe's photograph was taken by Penn Studio in the 900 block of Pennsylvania Avenue.

William Ashbie Hawkins was one of Baltimore's first African American lawyers. Around 1905, he partnered with George W.F. McMechen to form the firm Hawkins and McMechen. In 1920, Hawkins founded the Independent Republican League, whose headquarters were in the 1100 block of Druid Hill Avenue. Hawkins ran for US senator, and although he knew he had no chance of winning against the incumbent Republican nominee, he hoped to inspire other blacks to run for office. This image of Hawkins was captured by noted African American photographers Jones Studio.

EXECUTIVE COMMITTEE

J. STEWARD DAVIS, Chair.
W. NORMAN BISHOP, Secretary
E. MAYFIELD BOYLE, Vice Chr.
Wm. H. LANGLEY, Treasurer
MRS. JENNIE H. ROSS
MRS. H. E. YOUNG
MRS. HELEN COOPER
MRS. IDA HILTON
ARTHUR M. BRAGG
HARRY A. VODERY
HARRY OWENS
DR. WALTER JACKSON
CARL J. MURPHY
DR. THOMAS
LINWOOD KOGER
LEO STEVENS
WILLIAM PROCTOR
DANIEL RICHARDSON
TRULY HATCHETT
HUGH M. BURKETT

STATE HEADQUARTERS

.INDEPENDENT REPUBLICAN LEAGUE.

1107 DRUID HILL AVENUE

BALTIMORE,   MARYLAND.

* * * * * * * *

FOR UNITED STATES SENATOR FROM MARYLAND

W. ASHBIE HAWKINS

Thise letterhead lists the members of Hawkins's Independent Republican League executive committee, including James Steward Davis, William N. Bishop, and Carl J. Murphy. Several members of the Mutual United Brotherhood of Liberty were also on the committee.

INDEPENDENT REPUBLICAN LEAGUE TESTIMONIAL BANQUET

TO THE

HON. W. ASHBIE HAWKINS

(lately Candidate for the United States' Senate)

TUESDAY EVENING, APRIL TWELFTH, AT NINE O'CLOCK

AT THE LYCEUM HALL

TICKETS, TWO DOLLARS PER PLATE

OFFICERS

J. STEWARD DAVIS, Chairman   W. NORMAN BISHOP, Secretary

WILLIAM H. LANGLEY, Treasurer

COMMITTEE

Mrs. Jennie Ross, 2047 Division St.	Mrs. Helen Muse, 933 Linden Ave.
Mrs. Mayme White 403 N. Eden St.	Mrs. Sarah Mitchell, 427 Somerset St.
Mrs. S. J. C. Ralph, 1725 Orleans St.	Miss Ruth Sewell, 331 N. Stricker St.
Mrs. Alberta Turner, 422 23rd. St.	Mrs. Lucy Loving, 950 Druid Hill Ave.
Mrs. Cora Watts, 431 N. Eden St.	Mrs. Torella Lee, 1938 Druid Hill Ave.

Mrs. George McMechen, 2007 McMechen St.

This ticket was for an Independent Republican League Testimonial Banquet at Lyceum Hall, on the corner of Biddle and Eutaw Streets.

Estelle Hall Young was one of four women on W. Ashbie Hawkins's Independent Republican League executive committee. She relocated to Baltimore from Atlanta in 1905 and married Howard E. Young, proprietor of Young's Pharmacy, at the corner of Druid Hill Avenue and Biddle Street. Howard was the son of Rev. Alfred Young and brother of musician and real estate developer Robert J. Young. Estelle was the president of Baltimore's Colored Women's Suffrage Club and the Colored Young Women's Christian Association. She was also an active member of the DuBois Circle and often hosted meetings at her home in the 1100 block of Druid Hill Avenue. Both Estelle and Howard were members of the NAACP. The organization gave her its Award of Honor in the 1930s for her years of fighting for justice and voting rights.

Sarah Fernandez Diggs, of 1900 Druid Hill Avenue, was a longtime civil rights worker and the second wife of Josiah Diggs. She was well-known in Baltimore's social, civic, and educational circles and was a member of the Baltimore NAACP. Diggs organized many fundraisers for the community and spearheaded NAACP membership drives. She served as the state chairwoman of recreation of the Women's Division of the Maryland Council of Defense, whose purpose was to improve the comfort, social, and leisure time activities of African American soldiers at Maryland's Camp Meade.

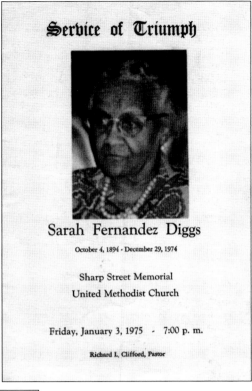

Service of Triumph

Sarah Fernandez Diggs

October 4, 1894 - December 29, 1974

Sharp Street Memorial
United Methodist Church

Friday, January 3, 1975 - 7:00 p. m.

Richard L. Clifford, Pastor

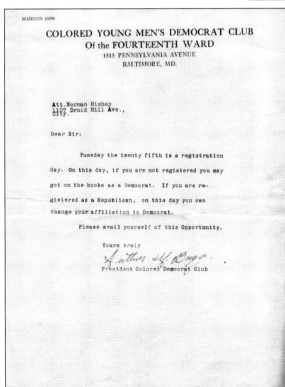

MADISON 10290

COLORED YOUNG MEN'S DEMOCRAT CLUB
Of the **FOURTEENTH WARD**
1515 PENNSYLVANIA AVENUE
BALTIMORE, MD.

Att. Norman Bishop
1107 Druid Hill Ave.,
City.

Dear Sir:

Tuesday the twenty fifth is a registration day. On this day, if you are not registered you may get on the books as a Democrat. If you are registered as a Republican, on this day you can change your affiliation to Democrat.

Please avail yourself of this Opportunity.

Yours truly
Arthur M. Bragg
President Colored Democrat Club

The goal of the Colored Young Men's Democrat Club of the Fourteenth Ward, in the 1500 block of Pennsylvania Avenue, was to encourage African American voters to register. Arthur M. Bragg, president of the group, was the son of Rev. George F. Bragg, the pastor of St. James Episcopal Church. He was the secretary of the Maryland Negro Democratic League and served on W. Ashbie Hawkins's Independent Republican League executive committee. Bragg lived in the 1400 block of McCulloh Street.

The City Wide Young People's Forum was established in 1931 by Juanita Jackson, daughter of Lillie Carroll Jackson, and presented its first program at Sharp Street Church, on the corner of Dolphin and Etting Streets. By 1934, the year listed on this program, it had over 500 members. Its goals were to provide a space for the black community to find solutions for their problems, to nurture the talent and potential of the city's young leaders, and to establish interracial unity. Other members of the forum included Clarence M. Mitchell Jr., who married Juanita in 1938, and Eugene Prettyman, musician and Boy Scout leader. Sarah F. Diggs served as the advisor of ushers. This 1934 intercollegiate event was held at Bethel AME Church and featured six historically black colleges and universities.

The Maryland Colored Democracy was in the 1400 block of Pennsylvania Avenue. The group organized mass meetings throughout the African American community to educate citizens about candidates running for office.

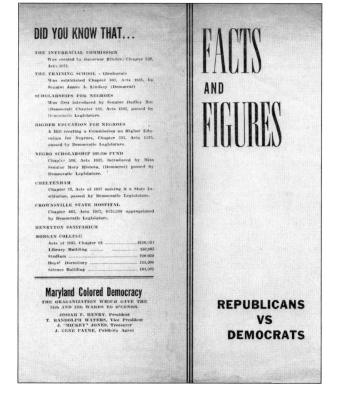

Rev. Edmond D. Meade (first row, third from left) was the pastor of Israel Baptist Church in East Baltimore for over 30 years. In 1937, Meade was the plaintiff in a lawsuit filed by NAACP attorneys Charles Hamilton Houston and Thurgood Marshall concerning housing discrimination. Meade attempted to purchase a home in an all-white neighborhood but was met with resistance. Although the case, *Meade v. Dennistone*, established that housing discrimination was legal, the NAACP did not have funds to appeal it to the US Supreme Court. Meade served on the executive board of the Baltimore NAACP for over 50 years and was called "Mr. Civil Rights." This photograph of him and members of his church was taken by E. Victor Wright.

This 1940 photograph shows the Maryland delegation to the National Colored Democratic Association convention in Chicago. From left to right are unidentified, Mrs. Lloyal Randolph; Lloyal Randolph, committee chairman; Eleanor Hicks; J. Gene Payne, liquor license inspector; unidentified; and Milton Dorsey, president of the Monumental Democratic Club.

The 43rd annual convention of the National Negro Business League and the National Housewives League was held in Baltimore in 1943. The convention headquarters was in the Masonic Temple on McCulloh and Mosher Streets. Charlotte Hawkins Brown was a speaker and a major draw at the convention. Willard W. Allen, grand worshipful master of the Masons, was the regional vice president of the National Negro Business League. The national director of the National Housewives League was Mary L. Beasley. This program was filled with local business advertisements and belonged to Ida Wilson Hayes, who lived in the 1100 block of North Carey Street.

New Voters waiting their turn to register at Court House. NAACP Vote Registration Campaign, November 1943

Baltimore Branch NAACP in ACTION

The Baltimore branch of the NAACP was in the 400 block of Dolphin Street. In 1943, it instituted a membership campaign with a goal of 20,000 members and encouraged people to register to vote. The front page of this pamphlet shows newly registered voters.

This early 1940s mural, "Negro Culture," was inside the old Dunbar Junior High School No. 133 in East Baltimore It was painted by Elton C. Fax, a 1926 Douglass High School graduate. Musician and fellow Douglass graduate Cab Calloway is on the right, standing in front of the wheel.

Back 'Em Up!

For a just peace at home and abroad

Join the . . .

NAACP

NATIONAL ASSOCIATION FOR THE ADVANCEMENT OF COLORED PEOPLE

Nationwide Membership Campaign 1945

Memberships $1, $2.50, $5, $10, $25, $100, and $500 Life Membership

This 1945 NAACP Nationwide Membership Campaign pamphlet was illustrated by Elton C. Fax. Both the mural and the pamphlet showed the local and national prominence of a Douglass High School graduate.

In this 1943 photograph, proud African American men are lined up to register to vote, with white election clerks in the foreground.

This voter's identification card belonged to Charles Robinson, a resident of the district. Such cards were required in order to vote.

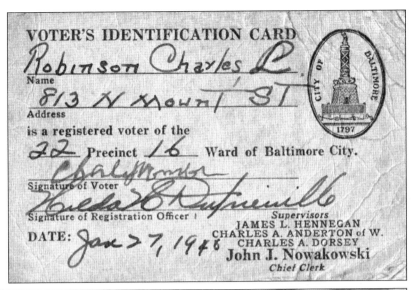

Pictured here is the family of Lillie Carroll Jackson. From left to right are (first row, standing) grandson Keiffer Mitchell, granddaughter Karleen Downs, and grandson Clarence Mitchell III; (second row, seated) daughter Virginia Jackson Kiah, daughter Juanita Jackson Mitchell, daughter Marion Jackson Downs, sister Florence Snowden, sister Marion Armstrong, and Lillie Carroll Jackson; (third row, standing) son Bowen K. Jackson Sr., son-in-law Clarence M. Mitchell Jr., Clarence M. Mitchell Sr., husband Keiffer A. Jackson, and son-in-law Calvin L. Kiah. This Old West Baltimore family is one of the most significant civil rights families in the nation.

Furman L. Templeton was the executive director of the Baltimore Urban League for over 25 years, where he focused on job creation, housing, and education for the African American community. Templeton also worked as the personnel manager for the *Afro-American* newspaper. He was active within the school system, church circles, and various clubs and organizations. He lived in the 1500 block of McCulloh Street.

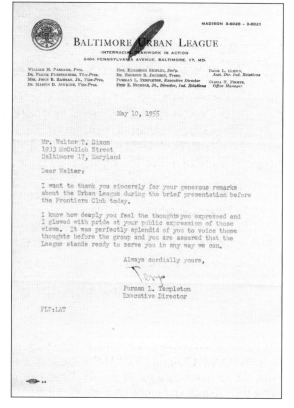

In this May 1955 letter to African American city councilman Walter T. Dixon, Templeton thanked Dixon for his kind remarks about the Urban League in a presentation to the Frontiers Club, a black service organization.

One of the most recognized attorneys from Old West Baltimore was Thurgood Marshall. No matter how successful Marshall became, he stayed connected to his hometown. His family lived in the 1600 block of Division Street. Thurgood attended the local schools and interacted with everyone. In 1946, he received the NAACP Spingarn Medal for his outstanding achievements in civil rights cases. Morgan State College honored him in February 1953 with a testimonial dinner and dubbed him "Mr. Civil Rights." Shortly afterward, he was one of the litigators in the landmark Supreme Court case *Brown v. Board of Education of Topeka, Kansas.*

A TESTIMONIAL DINNER

IN HONOR OF

Mr. Human Rights
"MR. CIVIL RIGHTS"

THURGOOD MARSHALL

sponsored by

Monumental City Bar Associaton

Sunday evening, February 15th, 1953
SIX O'CLOCK

MORGAN COLLEGE REFECTORY
Baltimore, Maryland

BALTIMORE BRANCH N.A.A.C.P. - 402 Dolphin St. - 17

Dear Member:

GOOD NEWS! **Hear CONGRESSMAN ROBERT NIX,** 1st colored congressman from Penna. Hear Baltimore's own **THURGOOD MARSHALL** tell about Little Rock . . . . this SUNDAY, SEPT. 28th, 3:00 p. m. BETHEL AME CHURCH, Druid Hill Avenue and Lanvale Street

MRS. MARGUERITE BELAFONTE, National Freedom Fund Chairman, will appear in person. GOOD MUSIC!

Do you want to help Little Rock? Bring your membership and tell your friends of this wonderful meeting! LOOKING FOR YOU!!

Dr. Lillie M. Jackson, Pres.   Dr. Carl Murphy, General Chairman

ANNUAL MEMBERSHIP CAMPAIGN NOW ON!
RENEW YOURS TODAY!

This invitation was sent to Rev. Edmond D. Meade to attend a historic Baltimore NAACP lecture at Bethel AME Church, Druid Hill Avenue. Thurgood Marshall spoke about the Little Rock Nine school integration case in Little Rock, Arkansas. The NAACP encouraged attendees to bring their friends and renew their memberships.

This April 1957 testimonial dinner at Morgan State College honored Carl J. Murphy for his dedication to civil rights. Murphy was the editor and publisher of the *Afro-American* newspaper, general chairman of the Baltimore NAACP, and a charter member of the Morgan State University board of trustees. He was awarded the 1955 Spingarn Medal for Achievement in Journalism. Grand Master William W. Allen, Thurgood Marshall, and Lillie Carroll Jackson delivered speeches at his dinner.

Lena Samella King Lee was an educator and attorney, and in 1966 was one of the first African American women elected to the Maryland General Assembly. In 1952, she was the third African American woman to receive a law degree from the University of Maryland, and in 1953, she was admitted to the Maryland Bar. Even though she was an attorney, she continued to teach at Henry Highland Garnet School No. 103 from 1947 to 1964. Lee was very active in community organizations, such as the Monumental City Bar Association, the DuBois Circle, and Sharp Street Memorial United Methodist Church, and was one of the founders of the Herbert M. Frisby Historical Society.

Verda Freeman Welcome was the first African American woman to become a Maryland state senator, serving from 1962 to 1982. Before she entered politics, Welcome was a public school teacher for 11 years at various schools, including Booker T. Washington Junior High School No. 130. As a senator, she was the major sponsor of a bill barring discrimination in public accommodations and helped to repeal Maryland's ban on interracial marriage. Welcome joined the Delta Sigma Theta sorority and the National Council of Negro Women because both groups were devoted to fighting against racism and prejudice within the community. The hand-drawn campaign sign below urged voters to elect Welcome to the House of Delegates, where she served from 1958 to 1962 before becoming a senator.

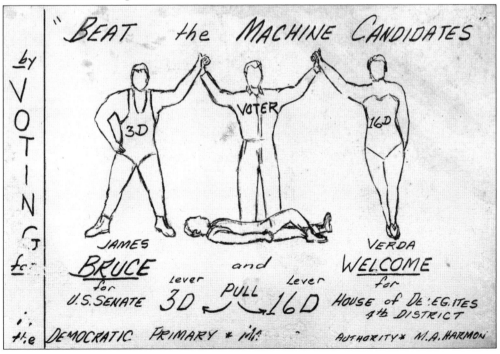

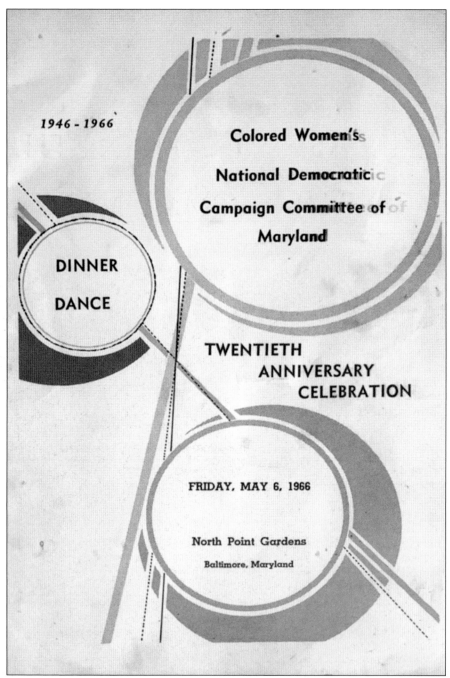

1946 - 1966

Colored Women's
National Democratic
Campaign Committee of
Maryland

DINNER

DANCE

TWENTIETH
ANNIVERSARY
CELEBRATION

FRIDAY, MAY 6, 1966

North Point Gardens
Baltimore, Maryland

Entrepreneur and pioneering African American Baltimore city councilwoman Victorine Q. Adams was the founder of the Colored Women's Democratic Campaign Committee. The organization, founded in 1946, encouraged black women to register to vote and run for public office. Their efforts resulted in the election of two firsts: attorney Harry A. Cole as the first African American in the Maryland Senate in 1954 and Verda F. Welcome as the first woman state senator in Maryland in 1962. This 1966 booklet was a 20th-anniversary celebration of the creation of the Colored Women's Democratic Campaign.

Six

PILLARS OF STRENGTH IN THE COMMUNITY

Rev. Alfred Young was born enslaved on Maryland's Eastern Shore. Young was a well-known minister who served at both Whatcoat Methodist Episcopal Church, Sharp Street Church, and others. He was well known for his "Railroad Sermon," where he told his parishioners to "catch the train for Heaven." In the early 1900s, he was manager of the Freedman's Saving Bank at 1200 Druid Hill Avenue, which had been established after emancipation to guide the economic development of African American communities. Young's children also became prominent: Dr. Howard E. Young was the proprietor of one of Baltimore's first black-owned pharmacies, Young's Pharmacy, and Robert J. Young was a musician and real estate developer. Reverend Young lived in the 1200 block of Druid Hill Avenue as well as the 600 block of Dolphin Street.

Josiah Diggs's life embodied the quintessential rags-to-riches story. He was the youngest child in a family of 18 and was orphaned at a young age. He worked odd jobs, saved his money, and purchased his first home on Druid Hill Avenue, which was predominantly white at the time. In the rear of his home, he started his wood, coal, and ice business and used the profits to open Baltimore's first African American–owned and –operated theater, the Dunbar, in East Baltimore in 1911. Diggs was a real estate developer and philanthropist who created the Josiah Diggs Memorial Charity Circle, which his daughter continued after his death.

Fannie L. Barbour was an early graduate of the Baltimore Colored School System, where she also taught for over 40 years. She was the English and mathematics teacher for over 30 years at the Colored High School, later renamed Douglass High School. When she retired in 1934, Douglass dedicated the 1935 yearbook to her. Rev. George Freeman Bragg wrote in the *Afro-American* newspaper that "the community can scarcely realize its indebtedness to Miss Fannie L. Barbour. She paved the way for a complete revolution in the educational interest of her race." She lived in the 1400 block of Madison Avenue.

Rev. Dr. Ernest Lyon (standing) was an educator, minister, real estate developer, author, and the US minister and consul general to Liberia. Lyon was the pastor at Ames Memorial United Methodist Church on Carey Street. In this photograph by Arthur L. Macbeth are John Lewis Morris, the Liberian secretary of the treasury; and John H. Reed, president of the Caroline Donovan Institute, created by the widow of slave trader Joseph Donovan.

Martha Eulalia Reed Calloway was the mother of musicians Blanche and Cab Calloway. She graduated from the Colored High School in 1898 and from Morgan State University. She became an educator in the Baltimore Colored School System and an organist at Grace Presbyterian Church at Dolphin and Etting Streets. Musical talent ran in her family: her mother, Annie C. Reed, and her father, Andrew Reed, were also gifted musicians.

Frances L. Murphy was the daughter of *Afro-American* founder John H. Murphy Sr. and taught at the Colored Training School for over 25 years. In 1926, Murphy suggested that the school be renamed the Fannie Jackson Coppin Normal School. In 1931, Coppin honored her with a testimonial banquet for her years of faithful service to the school.

Ida Rebecca Cummings dedicated her life to uplifting her community. Cummings was the first African American kindergarten teacher in Baltimore after she encouraged her brother, Harry, Baltimore's first black city councilman, to introduce an ordinance that established kindergarten in the Baltimore Colored School System. In 1904, she established the Colored Empty Stocking and Fresh Air Circle, which took the city's black children on summer trips to a nearby farm and gave them Christmas gifts. She graduated from Morgan State University, and in 1916, was elected the first female trustee. She organized the Frances Ellen Watkins Harper Temple No. 429, Daughters of the Elks, and served as daughter ruler for 31 years. She lived in the 1200 block of Druid Hill Avenue.

In December 1938, the Pride of Baltimore Lodge No. 713 and the Frances Ellen Watkins Harper Temple No. 429 held their 12th annual memorial service at Trinity Baptist Church. Ida R. Cummings was listed as daughter ruler.

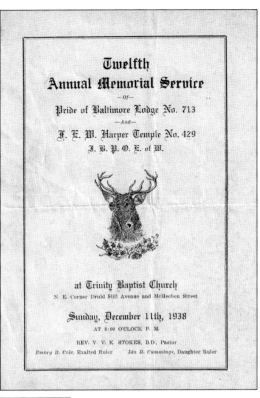

Maj. William Creigler (far right) was commander of Maryland's only African American National Guard unit for 20 years. Creigler was a World War I hero who was awarded the French Croix de Guerre. He became the first black major in Maryland history when Gov. Herbert O'Conor promoted him. Creigler lived in the 700 block of Dolphin Street.

William Henry Jackson Beckett (back row, fourth from right) was the first African American to receive a degree from the International YMCA Training School in Springfield, Massachusetts (now known as Springfield College), in 1906. He came from a prominent religious family; his father, John Wesley Beckett, was known as the "sweet singer" because his singing voice converted thousands to the AME faith, and his mother, Mary Campbell, was the daughter of AME bishop Jabez P. Campbell. Beckett was an athletic director and football coach at the Colored High School. During World War I, he was a lieutenant and physical education director for the Officers Training Camp for Colored Men in Des Moines, Iowa.

Leonard Ulysses "Duck" Gibson graduated from the Colored High School in 1910 and from the Springfield YMCA in 1915. His mentor, William H.J. Beckett, was the first black graduate of this college in 1906. During World War I, Gibson served as the athletic director at Camp Dix, New Jersey, and in France. In 1921, he returned to Baltimore, where he remained for 39 years as athletic director, coach, and mentor at his alma mater. When he retired in 1960, *Afro-American* sports reporter Sam Lacy dubbed Gibson a "Maker of Men."

William Llewellyn Wilson obtained his musical education at the Colored High School. He was privately trained by some of Peabody Institute's faculty because Peabody barred African Americans from attending. After graduation, he taught at Douglass High School for over 40 years, where he served as chair of the music department. At one time during the 1920s, all the music teachers in the Colored School System had been his students. He nurtured the musical talents of Anne Wiggins Brown, Blanche and Cab Calloway, Ellis Larkins, Ethel Ennis (whose middle name was Llewelyn), and many others. This photograph is by E. Victor Wright.

Josie Goodrich Smith was a longtime Baltimore Colored School System educator. Goodrich graduated from the Colored High School in 1914 and was mentored by Lucy Diggs Slowe. Smith taught and supervised a large percentage of the Colored School System during her decades-long career.

Dr. Frisby's success in being the second Negro to go to the North Pole, a boyhood dream, began when he decided to take his racist teacher's insult as a challenge. It took him 47 years to realize his goal, but he made it in a U.S. Air Force plane out of Eielson A.F.B., Alaska, under special U.S. Government orders, August 12, 1956, thereby giving world-wide recognition to the hero of his youth, Matthew A. Henson.

DR. HERBERT M. FRISBY

Arctic Explorer, Researcher, Lecturer
Sponsor—Matthew A. Henson Memorial Projects
Alaska, Canada, Labrador, Greenland, Spitsbergen
(European), Siberia (Russian) Arctic Expeditions

2nd Negro to go to the North Pole
(August 12, 1956)

3403 BATEMAN AVE., BALTIMORE, MD. 21216
Copyright, 1969

Herbert Milton Frisby was the second African American to go to the North Pole, making over 25 trips to the Arctic. He graduated from the Colored High School in 1905 and from Howard University in 1909. After teaching for 30 years, Frisby became principal of the Douglass High Night School and later taught at Coppin State University. In 1965, Delegate Lena K. Lee and a group of women founded the Herbert M. Frisby Society, dedicated to preserving Maryland's African American History.

Entrepreneur, financier, and political boss William "Little Willie" Adams (far right) is seen here with his wife, Victorine Quille Adams, and close business associate and friend Kenneth Bass. The group was returning from Chicago in 1942. Willie and Victorine married in 1935 at St. Peter Claver Catholic Church. Adams was known as a leading numbers runner and owned at least two nightclubs: Club Casino and Little Willie's Tavern.

Clarke L. Smith was an attorney in both Baltimore and New York. His wife, Bertha C. Frazier, was the sister of noted African American sociologist E. Franklin Frazier. Like fellow attorney J. Steward Davis, Smith also had both black and white clients. He was the vice president of the Douglass Amusement Corp., which was responsible for the construction of the Douglass Theatre on Pennsylvania Avenue, later the Royal Theatre. Smith also served as a member of the NAACP executive committee and attended St. James Episcopal Church.

Clarence Maurice Mitchell Jr. grew up in the Harlem Park neighborhood and learned to box at the Druid Hill Avenue YMCA. After graduating from Lincoln University of Pennsylvania, while working for the *Afro*, Mitchell witnessed a lynching. This inspired him to go into the field of public service and political activism. For the next 40 years of his life, Mitchell fought for the passage of crucial civil rights legislation, including the Civil Rights Act of 1964. This earned him the nickname the "101st United States Senator." He married Juanita Jackson, daughter of Lillie Carroll Jackson, in 1938.

Violet Hill Whyte was one of 10 children born to Rev. Daniel G. Hill Sr., pastor of Bethel AME Church. She graduated from Douglass High School and Coppin State University. In December 1937, she was appointed Baltimore's first African American female police officer. She retired in 1967 after 30 years of service.

Service of Triumph

FOR

LIEUTENANT VIOLET HILL WHYTE

1897 - 1980

Bethel African Methodist Episcopal Church
Druid Hill Avenue and Lanvale Street

TUESDAY, JULY 22, 1980
12 Noon

Dr. John R. Bryant, *Minister*

J. Gene Payne was an entrepreneur, liquor distributor, number runner, and president of the Monumental Democratic Club. He was the publisher of the *Red Book*, which listed the addresses of African American businesses in Baltimore. He was a World War II–era power broker and brother of attorney J. Howard Payne.

Longtime educator Betty Williams is pictured here when she was a student at Morgan State College. Williams was in the second graduating class of Dunbar High School in East Baltimore and was a 1944 Morgan State University graduate. For over 30 years, she taught in the Baltimore City School System. She was a longtime member of the DuBois Circle.

Parren J. Mitchell, brother of Clarence M. Mitchell Jr., graduated from Douglass High School and Morgan State University. During World War II, he received the Purple Heart for his service in Italy. In 1950, he sued the University of Maryland, College Park, for admission. In 1952, he became the school's first African American graduate student, earning a master's degree in sociology. In 1970, he was elected the first African American representative from Maryland in the US House of Representatives.

George L. Russell Jr. graduated from Douglass High School in 1946. From 1956 to 1966, he was an associate at Brown, Allen, Watts, and Murphy, an African American law firm, and was later named a partner in the firm. From 1968 to 1974, Russell served as Baltimore's first black city solicitor. In 1971, he was the first African American in the 20th century to run for mayor of Baltimore. He also served as the first black president of the Maryland Bar Association.

The author's great-grandmother, Gertrude B. Jackson, otherwise known as "Nanny Jack," was the matriarch of her family and a pillar in Sandtown. She was a midwife in the community, and her North Stockton street home was a safe haven for many folks over the decades. She is the namesake of the author's company, Nanny Jack & Co.

INDEX

DISCOVER THOUSANDS OF LOCAL HISTORY BOOKS
FEATURING MILLIONS OF VINTAGE IMAGES

Arcadia Publishing, the leading local history publisher in the United States, is committed to making history accessible and meaningful through publishing books that celebrate and preserve the heritage of America's people and places.

Find more books like this at
www.arcadiapublishing.com

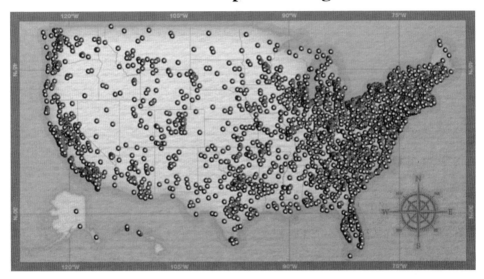

Search for your hometown history, your old stomping grounds, and even your favorite sports team.